THE SUCCESSFUL PROFESSIONAL CLIENT ACCOUNTING PRACTICE

THE SUCCESSFUL PROFESSIONAL CLIENT ACCOUNTING PRACTICE:

A Complete Guide to Profit Opportunities and Techniques

CARL S. CHILTON, JR.

Prentice-Hall, Inc.   Englewood Cliffs, New Jersey

Prentice-Hall International, Inc. *London*
Prentice-Hall of Australia, Pty. Ltd., *Sydney*
Prentice-Hall Canada, Inc., *Toronto*
Prentice-Hall of India Private Ltd., *New Delhi*
Prentice-Hall of Japan, Inc., *Tokyo*
Prentice-Hall of Southeast Asia Pte. Ltd., *Singapore*
Whitehall Books, Ltd., *Wellington, New Zealand*
Editora Prentice-Hall Do Brasil LTDA., *Rio de Janeiro*

© 1983 by

Prentice-Hall, Inc.
Englewood Cliffs, New Jersey

This publication is designed to provide accurate and authoritative information in regard to the subject matter covered. It is sold with the
understanding that the publisher is not engaged in rendering legal,
accounting, or other professional service. If legal advice or other expert
assistance is required, the services of a competent professional person
should be sought.

*From a Declaration of Principles jointly adopted by a Committee of the American
Bar Association and a Committee of Publishers and Associations.*

Library of Congress Cataloging in Publication Data

Chilton, Carl S.
~~The~~ successful professional client accounting
practice.

Includes index.
1. Professions—Accounting. ~~I. Title~~
HF5686.P89C47 1983   657'.834   82-15143
ISBN 0-13-868208-9

Printed in the United States of America

About the Author

Carl S. Chilton, Jr. has been engaged in public accounting practice since 1951. He is a partner in Long, Chilton, Payte & Hardin, a firm with four offices in the Rio Grande Valley of Texas and total personnel of approximately eighty people.

Mr. Chilton has written extensively on accounting subjects for many years. He is author of *Successful Small Accounting Practice*, published in 1976 by Prentice-Hall. He is a contributing editor to the *Practitioners Forum* of *The Journal of Accountancy*, and he won the Witte Award for the most useful article of the year.

He has spoken on practice management and tax subjects before state CPA societies in Hawaii, Washington and Texas, as well as before various other organizations.

Mr. Chilton is a past president of the Texas Society of CPAs, and has served the organization in many other capacities. He has been a member of Council of the American Institute of CPAs, and a past chairman of the Southern and Western Accounting Group.

He has been active in the civic life of his home community of Brownsville, Texas, serving as president or chairman of the City Public Utilities Board, United Fund, Rotary Club and Methodist Church.

Mr. Chilton is a graduate of The University of Texas at Austin.

What This Book Will Do for You

Almost all accountants serve professional clients: doctors, dentists, lawyers, architects, and others. Providing them with a full range of accounting, tax, and financial planning services is the central theme of this book.

Professionals make good clients. The accountant who learns to deal effectively with this group will develop excellent clients. They are interesting to work with, have challenging problems, can afford to pay for first class service, and are an excellent source of referrals.

This book contains many practical ideas, suggestions, and exhibits on how to provide a full range of services to professionals. Emphasis is placed on the need to be an adviser on a broad range of problems—to work with the client not only on tax and accounting matters, but on the full range of problems relating to practice management, investments, financial planning, estate planning, etc.

The techniques result from over 30 years of accounting practice by the author, including work with many professional clients. Ideas and material have also come from other practitioners in seminars and informal discussions.

The first two chapters tell how to help the professional organize his office. All phases of office management are covered—personnel, filing, collections, office controls and systems, etc. The point is made that most professional clients need and want more service than they are receiving from their accountant.

Chapter 3 moves into the area of financial planning for the practice. The importance of planning and budgeting is stressed, and a case study of budgeting in the professional office is provided.

The need to help the client select the right accounting system is covered in Chapter 4. Important features discussed are accounting requirements of various professions and the use of data processing equipment.

Chapter 5 discusses the needs of professional clients for audits or reviews, and highlights the advantages of an audit. Auditing professional clients is a service with more potential than is generally realized. A feature of this chapter is a discussion of clear and effective communication of financial information to the client.

Chapter 6 discusses the "bread and butter" service that usually brings the client to the accountant in the first place—income tax planning and preparation. This chapter discusses tax planning, tax shelters, use of trusts, retirement plans, IRS examinations, and related subjects.

Chapter 7 moves into professional corporations: the type of client who should (or should not) incorporate; advantages of incorporation; corporate retirement plans; how to set up the corporation; and how to operate the corporation on an ongoing basis. The accountant is given essential ideas and suggestions regarding this most important field of professional client practice.

Chapter 8 covers the broad range of services under general business advice. The accountant learns to help the new practitioner get started: how to get off on the right foot financially, how to get established in the community, how to arrange financing, how to set fees. Also covered are areas where experienced practitioners need help: control of productivity and workload; learning to delegate to others; keeping up with new developments; preparation for such problems as divorce, disability, and lawsuits.

Chapter 9 tells the accountant how to help professional clients operate successfully in a group practice. The chapter discusses the advantages of group practice, how to get started, how to select members, the right type of organization structure, and how to manage the group. It offers a variety of techniques for use in connection with the important matter of sharing earnings. Another feature is a discussion of how to bring in a new member, and how to arrange the payoff of a retiring or withdrawing member.

Chapter 10 deals with personal financial planning. It covers the need for setting financial goals, getting off to a good start financially in the early years, controlling personal expenditures, working with the spouse in financial matters, helping the client with investment decisions, and handling of financial emergencies. This is a higher level of service, where the accountant can provide much help to the client through his or her financial expertise and experience.

The final chapter covers the all-important area of estate planning. Many principles and techniques of estate planning are discussed, as is the human factor in this specialized field. The accountant has a central role to play in estate planning and this chapter provides tools to use in playing this role.

The message of this book is directed to all accountants dealing with clients who are members of other professions. Most accountants engaged in public practice will benefit from this material—not only in serving their professional clients, but in serving other clients as well. Many of the ideas and suggestions have broad application to clients in any area.

Most readers can particularly benefit from the advice to broaden the scope of their services. Many of us get too involved in the routine of meeting deadlines for financial statements and tax returns. We try to serve too many clients. We can't find the time to think in depth about client problems. The reader is well advised, therefore, to seriously study the material in this book about broadening the services offered—to give advice and assistance on the full range of the client's financial affairs.

Those who study these pages will be able to provide a more effective and wider range of services for their professional clients.

Carl S. Chilton, Jr.

Acknowledgments

When I write about the practice of the profession in which I have been engaged for thirty years, the thought comes to mind that there are many, many people who have contributed to the experiences that make this book possible. I shall always be grateful for the opportunity to be a part of the busy, sometimes hectic, and always stimulating world of the public accountant. The challenges, problems, and excitement are an important part of my life; particularly the camaraderie and give-and-take with clients and professional colleagues.

This book is a product of dealing with several groups of people over the years, all of whom contributed to my knowledge and experience:

Clients—They gave me the opportunity to serve them and confronted me with challenges and problems from which I learned.

Colleagues in my firm—My partners and staff have always been supportive and helpful in many ways.

Other colleagues in the accounting profession—Many friends among the fine people in the accounting profession have shared their knowledge and experience freely.

Other advisers to mutual clients—Working with lawyers, bank officers, insurance advisers, and others has always been a rewarding and stimulating experience.

I particularly want to express appreciation to my wife, Ruth, for supporting my urge to write and for being patient and understanding during many hours I spent at the typewriter.

My editor at Prentice Hall, Zeke Kilbride, has been a joy to work with. Not only has he encouraged and motivated me, he has reviewed my manuscripts promptly! The world would be a better place for writers if there were more editors like Zeke.

Finally, to the female accountants who read this book, any reference to the accountant as "he" is simply a term used in trying to communicate effectively. I wish I knew a term that would express the fact that both men and women are an important part of the profession. I have the highest respect for the talent and dedication of the woman accountants with whom I have worked.

C.S.C., Jr.

Contents

Table of Exhibits

THE SUCCESSFUL
PROFESSIONAL CLIENT
ACCOUNTING PRACTICE

1

Reviewing the Professional Client's Accounting, Office Management, and Records Requirements

PROFESSIONALS—A GROWING GROUP OF CLIENTS

An important part of any community is its professional men and women—doctors, dentists, lawyers, architects, accountants and others. These professionals provide vital services in keeping the community functioning smoothly. They are a hard-working group, dedicated to serving their clients and patients well.

The accountant frequently has the opportunity to serve members of other professions in accounting and tax work. They are good clients, are interesting to work with, have a good income, can pay appropriate fees, and are a good source of referrals because of their influence in the community.

It should also be noted that this is a growing field of service. The number of people in service occupations in our country is continually growing as a percentage of the total working population. The number of professional practitioners is likewise growing. Most communities today have more doctors, lawyers, and other professionals engaged in more varied fields of practice than ever before. This is a trend that seems destined to continue as various fields of knowledge continue to grow.

EXPANDING SERVICES THE ACCOUNTANT CAN OFFER PROFESSIONAL CLIENTS

Professional clients normally come to the accountant for help with income taxes. They need an accounting system to provide information for tax reporting. They need someone to prepare their income tax returns. They need someone to give tax advice and to answer tax questions. They often feel, however, that they have no need for additional accounting services and, in many cases, think their accountant can do no more for them. Unfortunately, the average doctor, lawyer, or architect is woefully unaware of the range of services his or her accountant can provide, and will continue to be so unless educated by the accountant. Otherwise, these professionals may go for years looking upon the accountant as a "necessary evil," whose only function is to keep them out of trouble with the tax collector.

The accountant must think in broad terms about the services he or she can provide professional clients. If services are limited to setting up an accounting system and preparing tax returns the accountant is shortchanging both himself and his clients. The concept of accounting services must be expanded. He or she must think in terms of general business advice, financial management, estate planning, and review of investments. A sincere interest in the clients' economic well-being is essential, as is in-depth knowledge of their business and financial affairs.

A survey by Richard J. Vargo, Ph.D., and Robert E. McGillivray, Ph.D., CPA, clearly highlights the need for broader services to health care professionals. Drs. Vargo and McGillivray are professors of accounting at the University of Texas at Arlington, Texas. They reported on their survey in the Journal of Accountancy, and the survey is reproduced as Exhibit 1-1 with their permission. Of particular interest is the significant number of health care professionals desiring additional services of various types.

One well-known accountant has observed that many fellow practitioners are "product oriented" rather than "service oriented." This means they concentrate on the product—the tax return or the financial statement. The concentration, however, should be directed toward helping the client run his or her business better. Financial statements and tax returns are obviously a part of our stock in trade, but they should not become the end result of our work.

This accountant further observes that while clients are willing to pay for products, they are willing to be much more generous in paying for help in running their businesses, increasing their earnings, and managing their investments.

A broader concept of service is, therefore, a key to developing a successful practice with professional clients. This concept is illustrated in the following example:

Bob Schaeffer, CPA, has been the accountant for Dr. Phil Hardin for several years. When Phil started his practice he employed Bob to set up his accounting system and prepare his tax return.

In his first year of practice Phil had some personnel problems. Bob got involved in this because Phil's secretary was having trouble with the books. When Phil decided to replace the secretary Bob helped him locate a new one. Bob interviewed and tested the new secretary, after which Phil made the final decision to hire her. During this period of personnel problems Bob assisted Phil in setting up personnel policies, and advised him regarding employee relations. Personnel matters have run much more smoothly ever since.

In those early years Bob assisted Phil with billing and collection policies, and helped set up a better office filing system when some problems began to develop there. As the practice grew, the manual accounting system couldn't keep up, so they looked at write-it-once systems and bookkeeping machines, and ultimately installed a bookkeeping machine.

A simple budgeting system for keeping abreast of office expenses was installed. Phil says this gives him a good handle on what his expenses should be.

The practice is now reaching a point where Phil and Bob are looking at incorporation, and adoption of a corporate retirement plan. They are also considering the idea of Phil's buying his own office building and leasing it to the corporation.

There is more work in the future in the fields of estate planning, analysis of investments, and other areas as the team of Phil and Bob works together on a broad range of tax, financial, and business problems.

SERVICES RENDERED BY NONACCOUNTANT PRACTITIONERS

The accountant should recognize that there is considerable competition for the professional client's work—some of it from practitioners who are not accountants. Some firms are specialists in serving the business and financial needs of a particular profession, particularly in the medical field. Many firms specialize in medical management, serving only that profession, and developing a true expertise in that field.

Some specialists work with the accountant, preferring to have him or her do the tax work. Others, however, insist on handling all the client's work, thereby leaving the accountant without a client. In this situation the accountant who has developed a broad concept of his services will be in a stronger position to retain the client. The accountant has the advantage of expertise in the tax and accounting fields, and a thorough knowledge of the client's affairs. Furthermore, the accountant is generally close at hand, whereas the specialist is likely to be from out of town.

It should be recognized that such specialists develop expertise in certain areas that are beyond the normal scope of the accountant. An example of this is advising on procedures for billing health insurance companies and the government for medical services. While the accountant with a sizable number of clients could develop such a specialty, this is not generally the case. The accountant should, therefore, recognize his limitations and be prepared to recommend a specialist when he observes the need. There is no reason why the accountant and the specialist cannot work together for the client's good when the situation requires it.

WHY PROFESSIONAL CLIENTS HAVE PROBLEMS IN THEIR OFFICES

Professional clients have achieved success because of education and experience in their fields. Their efforts have been and are devoted to keeping up with the demands of clients or patients. They normally have little interest or training in office management, accounting systems, taxes and financial affairs in general. They have great demands on their time and are able to devote only a limited amount of time to business and financial problems. Taxes are a subject that they would rather ignore.

FOUR PROBLEM AREAS IN WHICH THE ACCOUNTANT CAN BRING EXPERTISE INTO PLAY FOR THE CLIENT'S BENEFIT

The accountant's first job is frequently a process of education. He or she must get the client to understand the importance of accounting, controls, and office management. The client must understand that these are essential to a smooth practice, and must take some personal interest in these areas. The accountant should explain some of the problems (described in the following paragraphs) that can arise when these areas are disregarded.

1. Billing Problems

A poor bookkeeping system can cause difficulties in billing for services rendered. There may be a failure to accumulate all the charges that should be billed, or they may be charged to the wrong patient or client. Billings may be overstated or understated. There may be a delay in getting billings prepared, which will result in a poor cash flow.

2. Collection Problems

A poorly organized office and accounting system can result in collection problems. A disorganized office generally does a poor job of follow-up on delinquent accounts. The client may not even know the age of the receivables due to poor records or a poor system of reporting delinquent accounts to him or her.

3. Problems with Expenses

A client with a poor accounting system can let expenses get out of line and be unaware of it. A failure to budget expenses or to compare expenses with those of the preceding year leaves the client operating in the dark. He or she has no measure with which to judge expenses.

4. Accounting and Office Controls

Most professional practices handle a substantial amount of money. In some cases sizable amounts are received in cash. It is not unusual to find that the system of internal controls can be described as somewhere between poor and nonexistent. The client does not understand the importance of controls and the office staff is usually small in number, making it difficult to separate record-keeping responsibilities from the handling of cash. The problem is aggravated because methods of interviewing and screening new employees are frequently haphazard. The professional is, therefore, vulnerable to the possibility of embezzlement. Office personnel are tempted when opportunities are presented by poor controls. The fact that the employer earns a substantial income often increases the temptation.

Five Sure Symptoms of a Lack of Internal Controls

1. Cash disbursements are made directly out of daily cash receipts.
2. Checks are signed without reviewing supporting invoices.

3. Cash receipts are not deposited intact each day.

4. Prenumbered business forms are not in use.

5. The petty cash fund is not on an imprest system.

One experienced accountant thinks doctors are more susceptible to embezzlement than other professionals. This is due to the large number of individual patients handled by many doctors, the receipt of cash payments rather than checks from patients, the small office staff, and the lack of supervision.

The professional client is frequently reluctant to prosecute an embezzler after the act is discovered. He feels the publicity would be bad for his image and would rather not bruise his ego by letting the community know he has been taken. This makes it possible for the embezzler to go to work for another professional and have the same opportunity over again.

The professional client can provide effective internal control by devoting a minimum amount of personal time to it. One dental firm that lost several hundred dollars due to embezzlement in the early years of practice has set up a monthly meeting to check things over. The two dentists meet with the two office assistants and go over every active account. The following items must be in order.:

1. Do balances of patients receivable accounts agree with the control?

2. Do payments received match the agreed payment schedule?

3. Is appropriate follow-up being made on all delinquent accounts?

4. Are patients honoring their financial agreements?

The monthly two-hour session gives them an opportunity to discuss all their patients, good and bad, with the staff, and to give instructions on how to handle certain cases. It provides good communication between the staff and the dentists and improves staff morale.

One of the dentists personally makes up all bank deposits. When doing this he checks to see that the deposit slip equals the daily cash proceeds and the amounts credited to the individual patient ledger cards.

This is an example of how these professionals protect their own interests with a minimum amount of time. Not everyone will handle it in the same way, but all professional clients should be encouraged to take a personal interest in the financial and control features of their offices.

MINIMUM INTERNAL CONTROL PROCEDURES THAT SHOULD BE ADOPTED IN A PROFESSIONAL OFFICE

1. A double-entry system for cash receipts and disbursements tied in with the monthly bank reconciliation.

2. Daily deposit of all cash receipts intact.

3. All disbursements made by check with the professional signing his own checks.

4. Use of an imprest petty cash fund.

5. Accounts receivable records balancing with a control that ties into the system of charges and payments from patients or clients.

6. A monthly aged list of accounts receivable.

CONCLUSION

Good accounting and office controls are essential in many ways. Tax reporting requires good records. So does good financial management. These provide opportunities for tax saving and tax planning. Budgeting and planning of financial affairs require good records and office controls.

The accountant's challenge—and responsibility—is to see that accounting controls and office management are properly designed and functioning effectively. With that as a base, he or she can guide the client into more advanced tax and financial planning. The following chapters of this book will explain how to accomplish these objectives.

Most health care professionals require assistance in managing their practices and personal affairs. Both CPAs and non-CPAs offer management services to health care professionals, but CPAs are more numerous, more available (particularly in less populated areas) and, for most services, more knowledgeable, than non-CPA consultants.

To determine the range of CPA services to health care professionals and the satisfaction with those services presently being offered, questionnaires were sent to a random sample of 500 physicians, 500 dentists, and 400 veterinarians practicing in Texas.

Of the 651 health care professionals responding to the questionnaire, 87.1 percent, or 567 doctors, used CPAs for some aspect of managing their practices or personal affairs. The doctors' opinions of the quality of professional services indicated that 46.4 percent were definitely satisfied, 43.9 percent were generally satisfied and 6.7 percent were sometimes satisfied. Only about 3 percent were generally unsatisfied, definitely unsatisfied, or gave no response. These figures show overwhelming satisfaction with the quality of management services being provided to health care professionals.

Table 1, p. 28, shows services being offered by CPAs to health care professionals and the additional services that health care professionals said they would utilize and pay for if their CPAs provided them.

The preparation of income tax returns, income tax planning, and the preparation of periodic financial statements clearly constitute the bulk of CPA services to this group of health care professionals. These three services, plus accounting system reviews, internal control of cash reviews, and assistance with organizational form are the only management services that satisfy more than 50 percent of the demand for these services on a composite basis.

Table 1 also shows that these health care professionals desire a number of additional management services and indicates the relative degree to which CPAs are fulfilling the health care professionals' perceived needs for these additional services. Both the absolute and relative figures were reviewed since they indicated different aspects of the health care professional-CPA relationship.

The study shows an underutilization of CPAs by the health care professionals queried. Study of the use of individual services indicates that there is a wide variance in the use of CPAs by the various segments of the health care profession participating in this study. For example, physicians are receiving more professional services than either veterinarians or dentists. Dentists, in particular, are receiving fewer services from CPAs than the other two health care groups. It appears, for example, that few CPAs are assisting dentists with the installation and periodic evaluation of their insurance form processing system. Given the tremendous recent increase in dental insurance coverages, this professional service area should not be overlooked.

In short, the study reveals that while almost 90 percent of the Texas health care professionals responding to the questionnaires engage CPAs, and that almost the same percentage are satisfied with CPA services received, there are many additional management services that health care professionals, especially dentists, would like to receive from their CPAs.

CPAs practicing in states other than Texas should determine if all of the professional services can be offered in their local jurisdictions before proposing such services to their health care professional clients.

Exhibit 1-1: Survey of Use of CPAs by Health Care Professionals

TABLE 1

Professional Service	Service Used	Additional Services Desired
Income tax returns	566	9
Income tax planning	353	104
Periodic financial statement preparation	341	54
Accounting systems review	172	95
Review of investments	127	175
Internal control of cash	85	70
Estate planning	72	108
Cost control reviews	71	126
Receivable collection problems	66	110
Organizational form considerations	57	45
Review of insurance needs	53	114
Budgeting	51	108
Personnel management	46	64
Obtaining financing	43	74
Insurance form processing systems	20	60
Office location analysis	17	48
Patient scheduling system review	9	46
Office layout and decor analysis	7	33

Exhibit 1-1: Survey of Use of CPAs by Health Care Professionals
(Continued)

2

Helping Your Client Manage an Office and Improve the Accounting System

In a professional practice, more than in other types of business, an efficient office is the key to a smooth operation. To a large extent the office is where the action is, where the revenue is earned. The office, therefore, must operate efficiently and smoothly; the personnel must be well trained; and the system must be organized. This chapter discusses these and other aspects of office management, providing the accountant with ideas for serving the client.

HELPING THE CLIENT WITH OFFICE PERSONNEL

One of an accountant's important services is helping professional clients locate, employ, and train capable office personnel. The accountant has the experience to evaluate their qualifications, and knows where to locate prospective employees and how to interview and test their qualifications. The accountant should, however, limit these efforts to general office personnel of the client. He or she should not attempt to evaluate personnel who have training and expertise in the client's professional field.

The accountant may need to take responsibility for training personnel, primarily in the accounting function. Some time spent in training can save a lot of headaches later. The bookkeeper is taught the right methods early, with a follow-up to see that they are being properly used.

Setting Up Personnel Policies

The professional client frequently knows nothing about the importance of setting up personnel policies. The accountant can guide him or her in this area. If the accountant's own firm has written personnel policies, these can be used as a basis for assisting the client. The client should be strongly urged to develop complete personnel policies and to put them in writing. Exhibit 2-1 provides an example.

Closely related to personnel policies is the matter of employee relations, another area where the client can generally use help. This is particularly true where the client is an inexperienced practitioner. It takes skill and experience to develop a smoothly working office staff. If the accountant is in frequent contact with the client, he can spot problems areas and help smooth them out. The client should be briefed on some of the satisfying and unsatisfying factors making up the work environment for the employee.

HELPING TO DECIDE ON OFFICE EQUIPMENT AND SYSTEMS

The type of accounting system used by the professional client will be a key element in the successful functioning of the office and internal controls. In installing or improving the system, the accountant should follow certain basic premises. First, if the client has a system that is functioning smoothly and provides proper controls, don't change it. Equally important: keep the system as simple as possible. Resist the temptation to make it overly complicated. A simple system is better understood by the client and his people, requires less time and expense to operate, and is less likely to develop problems.

If, on the other hand, the client's office is having problems, a systems change may be in order. There are certain points to watch for that indicate problems in an office. Here are a few:

1. Books are behind and financial statements late.

2. Confusion exists among office personnel as to their duties and responsibilities.

3. There are undue increases in office personnel and expenses.

4. There are problems keeping up to date with billings, collections, and paying bills.

5. Inability to get appropriate information on accounts receivable, cash, etc.

In reviewing the client's system, consideration should be given to the various types of office equipment and systems that are available.

PROS AND CONS OF THE VARIOUS ACCOUNTING SYSTEMS.

A. Manual System. It has the advantage of being easy to understand and operate. The client can understand his own records if he wants to look them over. It is easy to train new personnel. The disadvantage is that posting of any volume of transactions can be a time-consuming burden. Many small professional offices, however, can get along quite well with a manual system.

B. Write-It-Once System. This is a manual system with features that enable the posting of transactions to more than one record at the same time. It is faster than a manual system and works very nicely when properly set up and operated. Some companies have developed sophisticated write-it-once systems that enable preparation of lists of outstanding accounts receivable and other data as a byproduct of the basic posting to the books.

C. Bookkeeping Machines. A bookkeeping machine is a valuable piece of equipment for posting of accounts receivable and other records when the volume of transactions increases.

When the client's personnel are continually behind a bookkeeping machine should be seriously considered. Keep in mind, however, that the operator must be properly trained and there can be problems if there is a turnover of personnel.

D. Data Processing Equipment. This equipment can be used by many practitioners, firms, and group practices to great advantage. The advantages and disadvantages are generally well known to all accountants. A great deal of data can be processed efficiently and much useful information can be generated. The installation of a data processing system is a specialized job, as is its operation. Such equipment should be considered only where the practice is large enough to justify the cost and the personnel.

USE OF SERVICE BUREAUS

A convenient substitute for data processing system or bookkeeping machine is the use of an outside service bureau. This lends itself especially well for processing customer's ledgers and accounts receivable billing, as well as such operations as job cost records for architects and engineers.

Three Key Factors to Consider

When considering the more sophisticated systems the client should be cautioned about getting carried away. It's easy to conclude that the present system is archaic and should be replaced by one that is faster and provides more information. Before making the move, however, it's important to stop and ask some questions.

1. Is the present system really that bad, or is it working reasonably well? Could it be streamlined with a few minor changes?
2. How will the staff react to the change?
3. What effect will the change have on relations with patients or clients?

When going to a data processing system or a service bureau it is especially important to have a complete understanding of the changes that will take place. Some professionals have gone this route and quickly become disillusioned. They have lost valuable employees because of difficulty in coping with the system. They have found that having accounts receivable records prepared out of the office (in case of a service bureau) made it difficult to provide information to patients regarding their accounts, and actually slowed collections. Some have found that patients responded better and paid earlier when the bills were handwritten, rather than an impersonal computer printout.

A service bureau should be carefully checked out as to cost, reliability and promptness. A preliminary trial run should be arranged while still maintaining the old system. Present customers of the service bureau should be contacted to determine their experience.

Modern data processing systems are a useful tool in the right situation—generally, the larger the practice unit, the greater the advantages. The disadvantages enumerated above can be overcome with proper planning. The accountant has the background and experience to help a client evaluate the benefits of using such a system in the first place, and to see that the pitfalls are avoided.

GETTING HELP FROM SALESMEN

Getting help from salesmen who handle write-it-once systems, bookkeeping machines, and data processing equipment can be of great assistance to the accountant and the client. Salesmen know their products and can provide useful ideas in solving problems. Their primary function, of course, is to sell their products and their proposals must be evaluated with a critical eye.

HELPING WITH BILLING AND COLLECTIONS

As explained earlier, successful billings and collections are a function of the office and accounting system and should be considered when the system is installed. The system should provide procedures for timely, accurate billings and steps to be taken in collection follow-up. These latter steps should be in writing and should be followed strictly.

The accountant should go further, however, and provide ideas as to various techniques and procedures that will improve the efficiency of the system and improve collections. Some of these are discussed below.

Cycle Billing

Most professionals bill once a month, at the end of the month. When cycle billing is first mentioned, they will say it is for the big companies. Why bother with cycle billing for 350 statements?

The answer to this will probably come when the bookkeeper is sick for a week just when the bills are supposed to go out. This will probably happen just after a big income tax payment was due and the bank balance is low. Further, the temporary help that was hired can't understand the system or read the poor handwriting of the client.

There you have one good reason for cycle billing. It evens out the workload during the month and brings in payments at an even rate.

Cycle billing won't work for all professionals, however. The situation of architects and engineers is completely different from that of doctors, for example, but it is one option that can be mentioned in the right circumstances.

Adopting a Collection Policy

The client should have a clear policy regarding collections (see Exhibit 2-2). These policies should cover initial arrangements for the work, advance payments, progress billings, follow-up on delinquent accounts, and discontinuance of services.

The collection procedures to be recommended will vary from client to client and will depend on the client's profession and situation. The accountant can provide guidance in this area to all professional clients, and above all should encourage them to have a definite collection policy. Otherwise, collections will be neglected and become a bigger and bigger problem.

Cost of Carrying Accounts Receivable

The client should be educated that carrying receivables is an expensive proposition. Some simple calculations can be made to reflect such items as interest on the money tied up, bad debts arising from uncollectible accounts and the cost of preparing and mailing repeated statements, not to mention phone calls, letters and collection expense. To make the most impact on the client, prepare a simple chart such as that shown in Exhibit 2-3.

Keeping Up with Past-Due Accounts

If the client has a tray of 500 or 1,000 accounts all in alphabetical order he or she needs some additional procedure for keeping up with past dues. Thumbing through a large tray of ledger accounts is an inefficient and incomplete procedure. What the client needs is a way to tell instantly if the account is past due, and how old it is.

A data processing system will, of course, produce an aged trial balance. But what about those without data processing?

The accountant should be familiar with various systems that are available for marking past-due accounts with various colored tabs. Generally, it is best to divide the accounts into two trays, one for those that are current and one for past dues. The past dues can then be tabbed, indicating by different-colored or different-sized tabs how old the various accounts are. This is relatively easy to update each month and keeps the client and his staff informed on the status of all accounts.

Use of a Collection Agency

All professional clients eventually have accounts that must be turned over to a collection agency for action. There is a wide range and variety of collections services, and the accountant can help guide the client to a good one. Here are some questions that should be asked of any collection agency:

1. How much does the agency charge on the accounts it collects?
2. What kind of tactics does the agency use in its collection efforts? (Some may harass people to the extent that the client would be better off not associating with them.)
3. How closely does the agency work with the client's office personnel?
4. What services, if any, does the agency give besides collecting money? (Some provide credit reporting and other services.)

HELPING WITH THE FILING SYSTEM

As an accountant you may have had problems with your own filing system, which you can relate to those of your professional clients. How often is a tax return or a financial statement misfiled? Have you ever had a client come in for an interview and been unable to locate his file? These same problems occur with the doctor, dentist, lawyer and architect. In each office they cause a scramble looking for the lost material, giving everyone high blood pressure and making a distinctly bad impression on the client.

If your professional client has filing problems, it is likely that some of the procedures you have adopted in your office will be appropriate.

Numerical Filing System

A numerical filing system will be advantageous to any client. Alphabetical filing has serious limitations for any sizable number of files. With only 26 letters in the alphabet it is time consuming to keep files in alphabetical order. Further, filing errors can occur too easily between files with similar names. An alphabetical system is simply not as precise to work with as is a numerical system.

When the system is already set up there will be some resistance to change. It will seem to be a big job to change from alphabetical to numerical filing. It is best, of course, to make the change before the files become voluminous or, even better, to start with a numerical system at the outset. The changeover is not all that complicated, however. The alphabetical files are simply given numbers in their present order and new files are added by numerical sequence. A card system is needed, of course, for alphabetical listing so the file number can be looked up.

Use of Different-Colored Files

When there are several types of files in the office (such as audit and tax files in an accountant's office) it is helpful to use different-colored folders. In any professional office this color arrangement will facilitate accurate filing and will speed the location of files when needed. If there are already files in existence, they can be marked along the edge with colored tape while using the colored folders for new files as they are opened.

HOW TO PERSUADE PEOPLE TO MAKE CHANGES

An accountant frequently recommends to a client that changes be made in office equipment, procedures, and routine. Such changes often disturb the office personnel. There are times, in fact, when the change can't be brought about or fails because of resistance of the staff. The client must, therefore, be made aware of the possibility of resistance. The accountant should anticipate this on the client's behalf. Further, if the accountant is involved in installing a new procedure for the client he or she will have to cope with this resistance directly.

Why do people resist change? Here's what the experts say:

New ideas and procedures appear strange and full of uncertainties. People wonder if they will be able to make the change, if they will be able to adjust, or if their jobs will be in jeopardy if they fail. This feeling develops even when the proposed change is recognized as an improvement.

People have certain everyday routines that provide security for them. The status quo is familiar and comfortable. A change is upsetting and requires extra effort. Many people prefer the easy way and the path of least resistance.

Some people resist change because of the way it is introduced. They may feel that the old system is being unfairly criticized or the new is being crammed down their throats.

People may oppose change because of a sentimental attachment to the old way of doing things and a reluctance to see the old system discarded. At the same time, they may feel it will change their working relationships or require them to work with someone who is incompatible.

In introducing change, therefore, it is necessary to overcome some of the problems mentioned above. There are several ways to do this.

People are much more enthusiastic about new ideas if they have had a voice in their formulation. The first rule to follow, therefore, is to invite participation. If new equipment is being chosen, try to let the people involved have a voice in the decision. Staff meetings are a way to involve people in deciding to change office routine or procedures. Seek ideas and opinions; let people voice their objections.

People who take part in developing change are less likely to be critical of it and more likely to try hard to make it work.

A few other points in introducing change:

Be very positive about the benefits and advantages. Point out such things as less paperwork, less drudgery, less pressure, more interesting and more enjoyable work.

Don't downgrade the old policies and procedures that are being scrapped. People who have been working with them may feel that they also are being criticized or downgraded. In fact, the system was probably devised by some of the staff.

Be realistic in explaining what will be involved in the change. If it is going to be a considerable undertaking, let the staff know. Don't underplay the problems, or make it sound overly simple. Give them the straight story.

If possible, tell them of some other office that has made the change and the beneficial results.

SUMMARY

The services described in this chapter will help the client solve his or her problems—services your client will appreciate. The accountant who performs these services successfully will earn the client's respect and gratitude—and perhaps a few kind words of referral, leading to new clients. The work in developing the office procedures will likely be followed up with higher level services, such as estate planning and financial management.

PROFESSIONAL MATTERS

The Importance of Clients

The continued growth and expansion of our practice is essential to each of us. Our practice will increase by the expansion of our services to existing clients and the obtaining of new clients. We want our clients to be satisfied with, and even enthusiastic about, our work. They are our most consistent sources of new business through their referral of new work to us.

We want our work to be first class in every respect. We must never reduce its quality for any reason. Poor quality work will hurt our reputation faster than anything else; each of us should resolve that every job be performed in a professional manner.

All of us should constantly be alert for opportunities to sell our firm and offer its available services. Clients do not always realize the size of our organization nor the scope of our services. We should inform clients of these services by speaking of the firm with confidence and pride.

Professional Activities

All professionals are encouraged to join our professional organizations as they become eligible. The firm also encourages participation in activities of the professional organizations.

Our future growth depends partly upon contacts made by its staff members in business, civic, professional, and social activities. Partners and staff are encouraged to participate in these kinds of activities. All of us should constantly try to broaden our contacts in the business community.

Professional Education and Development

Partners and professional staff are expected to keep abreast of current developments in our field. Continuing education and development is a never-ending process—it extends throughout one's entire career.

THREE OPPORTUNITIES FOR CONTINUING EDUCATION

1. Firm training sessions.

The firm holds several training sessions during the year for partners and staff. Everyone is expected to participate and to serve as a discussion leader when asked.

2. Courses sponsored by the profession.

The profession conducts a great many courses each year and the firm will send partners and staff to these courses as appropriate. Every effort will be made to see that each member of the professional staff has the opportunity to attend one such course each year.

3. Other courses.

The firm encourages employees to continue their education by any means available. An employee who attends a college level course that is directly related to the employee's responsibilities in the firm is eligible to be reimbursed for half the tuition. Employees are encouraged to be alert for any other educational opportunities that are available.

Exhibit 2-1: Personnel Policies

COMPENSATION AND EMPLOYEE BENEFITS

Compensation

Pay periods are biweekly and run from Saturday through Friday of the second week. Pay checks are distributed on Fridays.

Salary arrangements with each employee are made by a partner on an individual basis and are considered confidential.

Overtime will be paid for hours in excess of forty per week. Overtime work must be authorized in advance by the partner in charge of the office.

Each employee's progress will be reviewed at least annually by a partner. Promotions and pay increases will also be considered at least annually.

Retirement Plan

All employees with over three years' service are covered by the firm's retirement plan. The firm contributes 5% of the salary of each eligible employee to the Retirement Trust. Employees are eligible to contribute voluntarily toward their own retirement, and are urged to do so.

Hospital Insurance

The firm has a group hospital insurance plan and pays the premium for coverage of all employees. Employees can cover members of their family under this group at their own expense. The firm will pay the premium for family members and deduct it from the employee's paycheck.

Life Insurance

The firm provides accidental death benefit coverage for members of the professional staff because of the traveling they do on firm business. Eligible employees can take additional coverage at their own expense.

Sick Leave

Sick leave will be allowed with pay when an employee is ill. There is no specific number of days per year that will be paid for, but each situation will be considered on its merits. Employees will be eligible for sick pay after 90 days employment; during the first 90 days they will have sick time deducted from their pay. Employees are expected to call in regularly during periods of illness to keep the office advised of their progress. Failure to do so will result in loss of sick leave pay.

Dues to Professional Organizations

The firm will pay the annual dues for the staff members in appropriate professional organizations. Costs incurred in the attendance of meetings of these groups generally will be paid by the firm. The dues, fees, and expenses relative to a staff person's membership in certain other business or fraternal organizations will be carried by the firm. A partner should be consulted regarding any specific questions in this area.

Firm Social Functions

In order for employees to become better acquainted with each other as well as to relax and have a good time, the firm sponsors get-togethers for all employees and/or their families

Exhibit 2-1: Personnel Policies (Continued)

during the year. Announcements of this type of gathering will be made as far in advance as practical.

WORKING HOURS, HOLIDAYS AND VACATION

Normal Working Hours

The normal office hours are from 8:00 A.M. to 5:00 P.M. (with one hour for lunch) Monday through Friday.

Holidays

Unless demands for service intervene, the following holidays will be observed when they fall on a regular working day:

> New Year's Day
> Independence Day
> Labor Day
> Thanksgiving Day
> Christmas Eve Day (close at 12 noon)
> Christmas Day

Vacations

The amount of paid vacation allowable is based on the employee's length of time with the firm as of June 1 of each year. Generally, the following schedule is applicable.

Less than one year	One day for each month of service up to 10 days maximum
Over 1 year, but less than 10 years	Two weeks
Over 10 years	Three weeks

Vacations should be taken between May 1 and November 1 as an office's work load warrants. Shortly before May 1, employees will be requested to submit their selected tentative vacation time so that scheduling can be worked out.

Time Off

Time off for reasons other than illness, professional meetings, or vacations should be made up. Employees will be excused for such things as illness in the family, funerals, and others; but such time off should be made up.

An employee called to jury duty will be paid for the time spent in this civic activity and will not be required to make the time up.

Overtime will be paid only when a person actually works more than 40 hours. For example:
> Monday—worked 8 hours
> Tuesday—ill (paid under sick pay)
> Wednesday—worked 10 hours
> Thursday—worked 10 hours
> Friday—worked 8 hours

Pay will be for 44 hours (36 worked plus 8 hours sick pay). All pay will be at straight time since only 36 hours were actually worked.

Exhibit 2-1: Personnel Policies (Continued)

INITIAL ARRANGEMENTS FOR PAYMENT

The partner responsible for the work will make appropriate arrangements for payment. The client should be given an estimate of the cost of our services and an explanation of when we will bill.

Advance Payments

We will require advance payment under the following circumstances:

1. Someone requesting services of a "one-time" nature.
2. Someone not known to us who is requesting a considerable amount of work.
3. Any other case where the client's willingness or ability to pay is subject to question.

Progress Billings

We will generally render monthly progress billings on all jobs in progress of significant size. Exceptions will be cleared with the managing partner.

Follow-up should be carried out along these lines:

Account 30 days old—send a past due statement, with a personal note requesting payment.

Account 60 days old—write a personal letter in a fairly strong vein requesting payment.

Account 90 days old—make personal contact with the client.

Account 120 days old—unless satisfactory arrangements have been made, turn the account over for collection.

Discontinuance of Services

We will from time to time have clients who get into financial trouble and with whom we have to go along. In order to hold this type of situation to a minimum, we will discontinue services to any client who has an outstanding balance over six months old.

Exhibit 2-2: Effective Collections Policies

	Per Month	Per Year
Interest on $5,000 at 15%	$ 62.50	$ 750.00
Uncollectible accounts	50.00	600.00
Mailing past-due statements at $1.00 per statement	100.00	1,200.00
Time involved in making follow-up phone calls, discussions, etc.	75.00	900.00
	$287.50	$3,450.00

The cost of carrying receivables for one year is 69% of the value of the receivables.

**Exhibit 2-3: Cost of Carrying 150 Past-Due Accounts Receivable Totalling
$5,000**

3

Developing Dynamic Financial
Planning and Controls
for the Practice

NEEDS OF, AND BENEFITS FROM, FINANCIAL PLANNING

Most professional clients have little training in financial matters; hence they have little appreciation for the importance of financial planning and controls. While it is entirely possible for a professional practice to succeed and prosper with little or no financial planning, any practice could do better with planning than without it. Planning helps the client achieve his or her potential; a practice unit needs to know what its potential is, to set goals and targets, and to provide the professional members with an understanding of where they are heading. In group practice this provides a distinct psychological advantage and gives the members a stronger feeling of unity, direction, and teamwork.

Professional clients may feel that their business operations are fairly simple in nature and that the necessary planning and controlling can be easily managed. There may be some truth in this, but experience has proven that systematic planning will give better results every time.

Need for Planning in a Growing Firm

Many professional practices are growing in size, and this increases the need for planning and controls. The larger the organization, the more problems there are in controlling it. Large companies rely heavily on sophisticated planning and control systems as part of their management technique. While the average professional practice could hardly be compared with these companies, reliance on planning and controls by these giants nevertheless sets an example to be followed.

Growth in the practice normally means there are more professional members. These professionals have joined in group practice in order to enjoy the benefits of size and specialization. Group practice can indeed be most beneficial, provided it is properly planned and controlled. The professionals must have a common and agreed-upon goal and objective; they must all have the same understanding of where they are headed and what they are trying to accomplish. They must be willing to give up some of their freedom and subordinate their individual desires, to a reasonable extent at least, to the general objectives and welfare of the group.

A system of financial planning is a very good way to approach working together as a group. Development of the plan provides an occasion to sit down together and plan financial objectives. The group probably has other objectives outside the financial area, and the financial planning session provides a vehicle for communication on all objectives.

Financial planning also helps the group in developing its organizational structure. Frequently, it will reveal situations where responsibility and authority guidelines are not clear, or where responsibility should be delegated to subordinates, thus relieving the professionals themselves. The organization is sharpened up and both management and professional performance become more effective.

Long-Range Planning

In guiding and educating professional clients, the accountant can also urge them not to neglect long-range planning. Long-range personal financial planning is essential to any professional, and will be discussed in Chapter 10. Long-range planning should encompass objectives that are personal and professional, financial and nonfinancial. It can deal with professional goals and objectives, retirement plans, and goals in life outside the professional sphere. The accountant will not be involved in all such planning, but can be the catalyst to get the planning underway.

Another aspect of long-range planning deals with the practice unit, or the firm. This, too, is part of the process of planning and communication between the professional members, of reaching agreement on where they are heading. It deals with such matters as what will happen when a member retires, what he will receive for his interest in the firm, and whether the firm should move into new areas of practice.

The accountant should recommend that his professional clients in group practice consider holding an annual meeting away from the office. Sometimes called a planning retreat, such a session is usually held in a relaxed atmosphere at a resort. In a setting away from day-to-day pressures, the partners can make plans for the coming year; they can discuss long-range aspects of their practice and new developments in their profession.

For many firms, this retreat is the single most important activity of the year. It provides an opportunity to put everything into perspective. It's the once-a-year opportunity to stand back from the pressures of the telephone, clients, and staff and ask "Where are we going?" "What are we really trying to do?" and "What have we accomplished?".

It's time for the firm to assess whether it's heading in the right direction, and where it wants to be in three or five years. It's an opportunity to compare progress with earlier planning, to discuss what's been done right and what hasn't. Such a retreat can provide striking benefits, and assure solid lines of communication throughout the year.

An article describing in detail how one accounting firm handles such a retreat can be found in the December, 1977 *Journal of Accountancy*, page 34.

HOW TO WORK WITH THE CLIENT IN FINANCIAL PLANNING

Working in this area requires careful planning and special considerations in dealing with the client and that client's personnel. This is an accounting service which the client has an option to use or not to use—a considerably different situation from that of other services, such as income tax work.

The first order of business is to convince the client of the need for the service. The preceding paragraphs of this chapter have outlined the reasons for, and benefits stemming from, financial planning.

One important point is the terminology to use in discussing the work to be done. The terms "financial planning" and "financial controls" can generally be used effectively. Clients can understand what these terms mean and usually will feel that they need them.

The preparation of a financial plan, however, is sometimes referred to as a "budget," "forecast," or "projection." The accountant should exercise some care in using these terms, particularly at the outset. To the client a budget may sound like something that will restrict his or her activities, cost money, and increase overhead. If this term is used, therefore, it should be described as part of the system of planning and controls. If the client doesn't like the term "budget," use something else. The terms "projection" or "forecast" serve the purpose just as well.

A successful planning program requires the accountant to deal very carefully with the client and the client's personnel. The psychological factors in such a program are vital to its success. It is necessary that the plan have the full support of the client—otherwise it will not succeed. Every person who is responsible for meeting certain goals and objectives must participate in the planning process. In a professional organization all the professional members should participate, at least in regard to matters that directly affect them or over which they have control. Preparation of the plan must be a joint effort between the accountant, the client and the client's key personnel. A plan prepared by the accountant and simply handed to the client and his people will either be resented or be ignored. Therefore, two cardinal principles must be followed: (1) obtain the full support and participation of the client and (2) insist that the client and his personnel participate in the planning process.

The first time a plan is prepared the accountant generally will be heavily involved. He or she should plan to reduce this participation in the future by having the client and his personnel take over as much of the work as possible. By handling more of it themselves, the client and the client's personnel will find the planning process more meaningful.

The accountant does need to stay in contact with the client to see that the system and procedures are being properly followed. He or she should not set up the plan and simply walk away from it, but should see that reports are being prepared promptly and that a new year's planning process is instituted at the proper time. The client may be preoccupied with other duties and not follow through if the accountant does not do so.

The accountant should also review the plan to see that it is realistic. Some clients tend to want to prepare plans that are unduly optimistic. Their plan will picture what they hope will happen rather than what realistically is likely to happen. An overly optimistic plan can have a negative effect when the results come. Appropriate review by the accountant will help avoid this situation.

FIVE KEYS TO A SUCCESSFUL FINANCIAL PLAN FOR A PROFESSIONAL PRACTICE

There are several key to success in the operation of a professional practice. Each of these areas will come under scrutiny in preparation of a financial plan. Their application will differ somewhat between the various professions, but in each case the basic elements will come into play. It is important, therefore, that the accountant have an understanding of the importance of each of these key areas so he or she can educate the clients and analyze their operations accordingly.

1. Utilization of Professional Time

The first key is keeping the professional staff productively utilized in work for clients or patients. Full utilization of professional time and talent encompasses several ingredients: having a well-rounded staff; having enough business to keep people busy; having appropriate scheduling techniques to avoid wasted motion and provide people at the right level to do the work; and keeping necessary records of the services performed.

Generally a professional's primary contribution to his or her firm is productive service rendered to clients. It is important that the financial plan include targets for each professional member, stated in terms of chargeable hours, billings produced, number of patients seen, etc.

Further, it is necessary to compare actual results obtained against planned targets. This should normally be done on a monthly basis. Thus, the firm as a whole and each individual is made aware of how he or she is doing in relation to the plan.

Productive utilization of professional time is a key ingredient for financial success—indeed, this is probably the most important element in determining financial results.

2. Control of Work in Progress

Work in progress is a factor in the practice of several professions. Some jobs stretch out over a long period of time and must be controlled.

The work must be moved along on schedule and not be allowed to drag out. Suitable records must be kept indicating the amount of time and money invested in the job. A reporting system should be designed that will indicate which members of the professional staff are getting their work out and which ones are not.

3. Control of Billings

Control of billings encompasses the billing of full value for work accomplished. This is particularly important where the billing is related to time and charges or to a subjective evaluation of the services rendered. Some professionals will perform better than others and, in group practice, a system should be developed that will measure the total billings of each member and, if possible, compare it to some objective standard. There is a tendency on the part of some practitioners to reduce or write down their billings for various reasons, and the system should measure the results of this action.

4. Timely Billing and Collection

This point is tied in to control of work in progress, and good controls will minimize problems in getting timely billings. The client should be educated that the firm's inventory of unbilled time and uncollected accounts receivable represent potential cash revenue to the firm. They also represent a substantial investment, and improvement in billings and collections will reduce this investment.

Professional clients should be educated to enter into billing arrangements involving retainer fees or progress billings. These arrangements are quite common on lengthy jobs, but the accountant should see that the client is utilizing it to the fullest extent.

5. Control over Expenses

The client should be made to understand that control of expenses has a direct effect on his or her net income. While this should be obvious, it is sometimes overlooked in the press of day-to-day business. In most professional practices expenses come to at least 40% of net income, much more in some cases. The client should develop an awareness of where this money is going, whether costs are higher than normal in that professional field, how much costs are going up in the coming year.

One of the most important steps in developing a financial plan is the budget of expenses. All past expenses of any significance must be analyzed and critically evaluated. A projection of the coming year's expenses should be made in sufficient detail to provide a basis for comparing the actual results with the projection.

CASE STUDY

This chapter closes with an illustrative financial plan prepared by a law firm, with the assistance of their accountant (Exhibit 3-1). The approach described could generally be used in working with clients in any profession, with appropriate variations in determining specific items. Working up the expense plan would be quite similar for all the professions, but the methods of determining revenues would vary. Further, some professions have direct job costs that must be considered. In any event, the budgeting techniques applicable to a professional practice are relatively simple, and, as pointed out earlier, the most important part of the engagement involves working skillfully with the client's people.

Wilson and Day is a twelve-year-old law firm offering a fairly wide range of legal services to a growing number of clients. It has grown from a two-man practice to a seven-man firm (four partners and three associates). Billings now exceed the $450,000 mark. The partners feel they can increase their earnings by developing a financial plan for the coming year, and have engaged their accountant to assist them. In the past year the firm collected about $460,000 in fees and distributed about $230,000 in profits to the partners. It has been decided that next year's net profit will be divided among the partners as follows:

Mr. Wilson	28%
Mr. Day	28%
Mr. King	24%
Mr. Baker	20%

The accountant has recommended that a profit goal of $320,000 be set for the next year. The partners agreed to this and further decided that Mr. Wilson would charge $90.00 per hour, Mr. Day would charge $85.00, Mr. King would charge $60.00, and Mr. Baker $55.00. The setting of billing rates is a matter of judgment, and is influenced by rates charged in prior years as well as by competitive rates prevailing in the area. In this instance, the setting of billing rates was the first step in the plan. Once the rest of the plan has been completed the partners may adjust the billing rates to achieve a more balanced rate structure or to achieve a different profit result.

Another approach is to first determine the operating expenses of the firm, then to set billing rates and determine estimated revenue to achieve the desired profit. Either approach is largely determined by personal preference and the end result should be the same either way.

The partners then decided that sufficient growth in business was anticipated to require the employment of an additional associate during the year. Once this decision was made, the billing rates of the associates were set and the revenues of the firm were projected as follows:

	This Year			Next Year		
	Chargeable hours	Billing rate	Billings	Chargeable hours	Billing rate	Billings
Partners:						
Wilson	1,200	$65	$ 78,000	1,100	$90	$ 99,000
Day	1,200	65	78,000	1,200	85	102,000
King	1,200	55	66,000	1,100	60	72,000
Baker	1,200	50	60,000	1,100	55	61,000
Associates:						
Watson	1,600	40	64,000	1,600	45	72,000
Boyd	1,600	40	64,000	1,600	45	72,000
Jeffers	1,600	35	56,000	1,600	40	64,000
New associate				1,200	30	36,000
			$466,000			$578,000

It was decided that Mr. Wilson's chargeable hours would be decreased so he could devote more time to the management of the firm, and that Mr. Baker's would be decreased since he

Exhibit 3-1: Preparation of Financial Plan for a Law Firm

was participating heavily in community affairs. It was noted that this participation would very likely bring new business.

A salary schedule was then prepared for the associates and other employees. The following salaries were agreed upon:

Associates:	
Watson	$ 30,000
Boyd	30,000
Jeffers	25,000
New associate	15,000
Four secretaries	44,000
Receptionist	7,000
Librarian/bookkeeper	10,000
	$161,000

The accountant pointed out that there should be a consistent relationship between salaries paid and fees produced by the associates. This was computed to be as follows for each associate:

Watson (salary as a percent of fees)	41%
Boyd	41%
Jeffers	39%
New associate	42%

It was decided that a 40% ratio was reasonable and that these percentages were in line. It was further decided that when the profit plan was completed this ratio would be reviewed again, if necessary.

BUDGET FOR OTHER EXPENSES

The accountant requested the firm's bookkeeper to prepare an analysis of all significant expenses for the preceding year, leaving a column to use for the coming year's expense budget. Mr. Wilson and the accountant then reviewed last year's expenses and determined the preliminary budget figure for the coming year. These are some of the things that were considered:

Rent. The current amount of space was reviewed, along with needs for the future. The firm already had sufficient space for the new associate, but arrangements would have to be made for additional space before any more people could be added.

Library. The present costs were reviewed and evaluated as to their need. Mr. Wilson consulted the other partners as to any additional library needs. An increase was budgeted to cover new materials in a field where the firm felt the library was deficient.

Dues. Each item was reviewed as to its justification. Dues in professional organizations were evaluated, as were those in community organizations. Some items were added and some were dropped.

Professional Meetings. Each partner was asked to indicate those he wanted to attend during the year and the proposed cost. A budget figure was determined for each partner's

Exhibit 3-1: Preparation of Financial Plan for a Law Firm (Continued)

participation. Recognizing the need for professional development by the associates, a similar procedure was used for their meetings.

Office Supplies. This is a significant expense category. It is difficult to budget by specific item because of the diversity of purchases made. It can be analyzed on an item basis, or can be budgeted as a percentage of gross fees. Certain questions were raised for discussion by the accountant, such as buying in larger quantities, preparing internal forms by use of firm copying equipment, etc. The accountant pointed out that it is easy to get into a rut purchasing supplies, and if the firm is alert it can find ways to save money.

Insurance. The amounts and types of coverage for the prior year were reviewed, and needs for the coming year discussed. The accountant recommended that the firm bookkeeper keep an up-to-date insurance register, making it easier to determine coverage carried and compare costs from year to year.

New Furniture and Equipment. New furniture was required for the new associate, and this was budgeted. Mr. Wilson also determined, after consulting the other partners, that some upgrading of the dictating equipment was needed, and a budget figure was included for it.

Total Expenses. Total expenses, exclusive of salaries, as determined by the accountant and Mr. Wilson, came to a total of $115,000.

Profit Plan for the Year. The profit plan for the year looked like this:

Fee produced		$578,000
Expenses:		
Salaries	$161,000	
Other expenses	115,000	276,000
Net profit		302,000

The projected profit came up $18,000 short of the $320,000 the firm hopes to reach. This result was presented to all the partners, who then reviewed the plan to see what could be done. It was decided that the most practical approach would be for each partner to get 60 additional hours of chargeable time, which would bring in another $18,000 in revenue. The revenue projection was, therefore, increased accordingly. It was noted that the expense budget would be difficult to reduce. There was, however, a reasonable chance that the associates would produce billings in excess of their budgeted amounts.

The conclusion was that the $320,000 profit target could be reached, but that a concentrated effort on the part of the partners would be necessary. It was further agreed that having such a target and knowing what was required to reach it would give the firm more incentive toward reaching their goal.

Exhibit 3-1: Preparation of Financial Plan for a Law Firm (Continued)

4

Designing and Improving
Accounting Systems
for Professionals

The accounting system provides the data from which the professional client's financial and tax decisions are made. It provides the raw material for the accountant to use in rendering other services—tax, financial planning, budgeting, etc. The designing and monitoring of the accounting system is an essential part of the package of services the accountant offers.

An accounting system should be dynamic and changing as the client's needs change. A professional practice will not remain static over the years—it will grow, occasionally it will diminish in size, the needs of the client will change, the type of the organization will change. The system itself must change so that it will continue to meet the needs.

The accountant will be required from time to time to design and install a system for a new client—and the primary thrust of this chapter is toward that end. An equally important job, however, is keeping an eye on the systems of existing clients and recommending needed improvements. This is easy to overlook. The accountant tends to become preoccupied with completing a tax return or financial statement, failing to be alert to deficiencies in the system. Don't get too accustomed to the same system, the same way of doing things, overlooking the need for improvements.

An important point to bear in mind: every system can be improved; watch for ways to improve each client's accounting system.

CONVINCING THE CLIENT OF HIS NEEDS

Many times the client doesn't understand what he or she needs in an accounting system. Many clients want a system that will be simple to operate and yet provide a multitude of financial data instantaneously. These requirements are, of course, generally incompatible. The client must be told that the more information he wants, the more complex the system.

Some clients look upon accounting as an overhead item and a nuisance. They want only what is required for tax reporting. In this case the accountant should analyze the situation to determine the client's actual needs. Most clients are not aware of the benefits of good financial reports. It takes some salesmanship to get this across.

If the client looks upon the accountant as a financial adviser rather than merely a tax preparer he will welcome recommendations regarding a broader concept of what the accounting system can do for him.

VARIED NEEDS OF PROFESSIONAL CLIENTS

The accounting systems of professional clients vary widely. The two principal reasons for this are:

- Type of professional activity.
- Size of professional practice.

The discussion that follows in this chapter will point out the differences in accounting system needs of the various professsions. Some of the varied requirements:

- Handling and controlling funds received in cash (doctors and dentists).
- Job cost accounting (architects and engineers).
- Accounting for trust funds (lawyers).
- Allocation of certain categories of income and expenses for profit sharing purposes (all professions).

In dealing with these varied requirements the accountant must have an understanding of the methods of operation in the profession with which he is dealing.

Professional practices range in size from one-man firms to those that are national in scope. Most accountants will deal with a considerable size range among their own clients; the larger the organization, the more complex the accounting system. In larger group practices the system will involve several considerations:

- Type of reporting needed for management and for members of the group (cash, accrual).
- Consideration of needs for data processing equipment.
- Consideration of special allocations required by profit sharing arrangements within the group.
- Cash controls and cash management needs.

OBJECTIVES IN DESIGNING THE SYSTEM

The objectives of the system will differ among clients. All clients will want a system that will handle tax reporting requirements. Most will want financial reports. Beyond these two objectives there are certain others that some clients will need and some will not.

The accountant must determine the objectives to be recommended to the client and discuss them with him or her. This discussion will provide a basis for explaining the requirements and benefits the client can derive from a particular system.

The following discussion provides the accountant with guidelines for determining which objectives to discuss with the client.

Control of Operating Costs. A prime objective of the system should be control of operating costs. This is an important point to mention to the client who starts out being interested only in tax reporting. Discuss the advantages of a monthly report of operating costs, particularly when used in comparative form with costs of the prior year or with a budget. Careful consideration should be given to the chart of accounts for operating costs, providing the allocation and breakdowns that best fit the client's needs.

Setting Fees. The accounting system should provide information that can be used in setting fees and preparation of billings. Medical practitioners will need a record of patient visits and services rendered. Professionals who bill based on time charged will need a time recording system and method of summarizing charges for billing purposes. In some instances the fees charged will be related to a criterion outside the accounting system, but even in those cases it is important to have control over the direct cost of rendering the service.

Tax Reporting. This is a basic requirement and the one the professional needs at the outset. The accountant must see that Internal Revenue Service requirements are met and the system will stand up in case of examination. Consideration must be given to proper substantiation of deductions, seeing that the majority of expenses are paid by check, etc. It is important that accounting for income, particularly cash, is handled so that the IRS will be satisfied that all income is accounted for.

Determining the Valuation of the Practice. In group practices with buy-out provisions for retiring or withdrawing members the system must provide necessary information to determine the price to be paid. The accountant should be familiar with the agreement and be sure the system will provide financial data needed to conform to it.

Division of Earnings. The system must provide for an appropriate division of earnings among members in group practice. This normally presents no unusual problems. As discussed in Chapter 9 on group practice, however, some groups have developed innovative methods of dividing earnings based on certain allocations of income and expenses. In such cases the system must provide a method of making these allocations efficiently and in a manner so that all members can understand the arrangement and are satisfied with it.

Financial Reports. The accounting system should provide information for preparation of financial reports. Such reports will include the basic financial statements as well as statistical and other supplementary data of use to the client. The system should make it possible to prepare such reports in a timely manner after the end of the accounting period.

Budgeting. For the client who is interested in setting financial goals through use of budgeting, the system should provide historical data to use as a starting point.

Management of Cash. Some professional clients have cash flow problems. Others have excess cash to invest. These clients need a system that provides for cash management—either when to borrow or when to invest excess funds, as the case may be. The system should encompass frequent reports of cash income and outgo, as well as projections of cash needs and points at which borrowing or investing is required.

Control of Job Costs. For those professional activities where job costs are a factor, control of these costs is needed. Architects and engineers incur a variety of costs in performing their work on various projects. The system should be designed to assign such costs to their specific project so the client will have current information regarding profitability.

Internal Controls. The system should be designed so that necessary controls are in place. The importance of internal controls is discussed in Chapter Five. In designing or reviewing the system the accountant must always be alert to the effectiveness of internal controls. Indeed, this is one of the basic and most important functions of the accounting system. In discussing with the client the benefits of a good accounting system the need for controls should be emphasized. Also, bear in mind that the system must be reviewed periodically—a good system of controls can easily become loose if the accountant fails to keep an eye on it.

Determination of Working Capital Needs. This subject is similar to cash management discussed above, but broader in scope. Working capital needs encompass the total needs of the client, including carrying of receivables and work in progress, financing equipment purchases, etc. The system should provide adequate information to analyze these matters and determine a course of action.

Management of Receivables. Most professionals have the same accounts receivable problems as do commercial businesses: they must do the necessary bookkeeping and collection follow-up.

One management problem in many small practices is poor receivables bookkeeping. The system is probably operated without accounting controls, so that errors go undetected. Some systems use loose cards or ledger sheets that can be misplaced. The accountant must impress upon the client that accounting for his receivables is important.

In addition to the routine accounting, the system must provide for reporting and analysis of receivables. The client should be given periodic reports on the status of receivables for follow-up. An analysis on a monthly or quarterly basis should include the following:

- Total fees charged and total fees collected.
- Percentage of fees charged that have been collected.
- Number of days' charges in accounts receivable.
- Accounts receivable aging.
- Determination of collection follow-up.
- Determination of accounts to be turned over to collection agency.

SELECTING THE RIGHT SYSTEM

Selecting the right system to install is vital. After the accountant has determined the client's accounting system needs, he is then in a position to consider the type to use. There are many options to choose from, particularly in the area of data processing equipment. A recommendation must be made only after due deliberation and consideration of all viable options.

Getting Help from Salesmen

Sales representatives of various manufacturers can provide much valuable data regarding types of systems available. The accountant should utilize their expertise, but should know how to deal with sales people. Keep in mind that their primary function is to sell their product; their proposals, therefore, must be evaluated with a critical eye.

Proposals should be requested from more than one company. This provides several sources of ideas and price competition. A limit should be placed on the number of proposals to be evaluated, however, since too many will present a burden. It is best to choose not more than half a dozen companies. The accountant will normally prefer to deal with the best known and established companies in the area, although newer companies should not be overlooked, for they are frequently innovative and anxious for business.

In deciding which companies to deal with, emphasis should be placed on their reputation for providing prompt and reliable service for their equipment. Data processing equipment is only as good as the service that goes with it, and out-of-service equipment creates problems.

All proposals received must be evaluated carefully. Be sure the salesman has spent sufficient time studying the client's needs to understand what is required. The accountant generally is more familiar with such matters as the number of transactions or potential for growth than the salesman, and should see that he understands such points.

Before making a final selection, discuss the installation requirements with the salesman. Let him know he is expected to spend sufficient time with the installation to see that it is functioning properly. Some salesmen move on to the next job and neglect the proper follow-up on installation. The point should be made that a thorough job is expected during the installation phase.

The sales representative will sometimes design forms to be used with the system. The accountant should review these forms to be sure they provide complete data and leave an audit trail. Do not permit installation of a system where certain data are stored in the machine and cannot be traced. This may be efficient, but will create problems at some point in connection with a tax examination or other audit. Be sure the system is complete and provides all required data in print.

Manual Systems

Manual systems will most likely be used in connection with small practitioners whose need for accounting data is limited. Such a system has the advantage of ease and simplicity of operation and of instructing personnel in its use. It is also easy to break the work into different levels, with people of different skills doing the necessary portions of the work.

The biggest disadvantage of a manual system is that it is time consuming and subject to clerical errors. These problems become particularly aggravating when using unskilled bookkeeping personnel. It is not unusual for the accountant to unscramble a poor set of records at a cost greater than would have been incurred to employ a more qualified person in the first place.

If the client uses a manual system the accountant should take steps to see that as many controls as possible are in place:

- A double-entry system that is balanced monthly.
- Monthly bank reconciliations tied into book balances.
- Balancing of payroll records and payroll taxes against the general accounting records.
- A chart of accounts to be used in classifying transactions.

A periodic review by the accountant of the record keeping during the year will help save time and problems at year end.

Pegboard Accounting Systems

Pegboard accounting systems are particularly well suited to smaller professional offices. Vendors of these systems have developed specifically designed forms and systems for various professionals that answer the need admirably. The accountant would be well advised to consider this alternative when installing a system.

Manufacturers of pegboard systems have designed forms that can be utilized in connection with a variety of accounting operations. Some of these are:

- Cash receipts.
- Cash disbursements.
- Employee earning records.
- Daily record of patients seen and charges made.
- Client or patient billings (Exhibit 4-1).
- Insurance company billings.
- Job cost accounting.
- Accounting for trust funds (Exhibit 4-2).
- Accounting for chargeable time.
- Appointment and due date reminder system.
- New matter report for attorneys (Exhibit 4-3).

Some advantages of a pegboard system:

- Requires discipline in keeping up to date.
- Requires daily balancing of receipts and bank deposits.
- Reduces clerical errors.
- Reduces bookkeeping time.

A pegboard system is more formal than a manual system, requiring that certain procedures be followed. There is less chance of the bookkeeper's falling behind or ignoring system procedures than in a manual system.

A pegboard system can provide the basic data for input into a computerized general ledger and financial reporting service. The accountant can provide the computer service using his own hardware or transmit the data to a company specializing in this type of service.

As with any system, the accountant must see that it is being properly followed by client personnel. For the system to function properly the procedures must be followed conscientiously. Failure to do so will bring on year-end problems similar to those discussed in connection with manual systems. It is important, therefore, for the accountant to be in frequent contact with the client, preferably reviewing the records periodically throughout the year.

Data Processing Systems

The current trend, and one which undoubtedly extends into the future, is toward increasing use of data processing equipment in professional offices. The field of data processing, continually changing as a result of dramatic advances in technology, poses a real challenge to the accountant in deciding on the type of system to recommend.

Data processing systems are continuing to improve and becoming more attractive to use in several respects:

- They are becoming more cost effective.
- Space and other physical requirements for the equipment are simpler than in earlier days.
- Software is becoming more readily available and more reliable.
- Equipment is easier to operate, creating fewer problems in connection with the need for highly trained personnel.

Some advantages to the client in using a data processing system rather than manual or pegboard systems:

- The system is fast and efficient in operation.
- It can accumulate all data necessary in connection with the practice, particularly statistics needed to analyze operations.
- The work is more likely to be up to date at all times.
- The system requires formal written instructions so that the operator is less likely to fall into lax practices.

Data processing systems are not without their problems. Some of the potential disadvantages:

- Need for skilled personnel, difficulty of recruiting and training (as noted above, this problem is now minimized in case of some systems).
- Possibility that the system may generate different data from that which the client wants, or generate too much data.
- Possibility that the system can get fouled up in a big way by input of incorrect data.
- Difficulty in evaluating different systems and equipment and making a choice between them.

The client has the opportunity to choose between several alternatives in data processing systems. Such systems vary from in-house hardware to on-line systems or service bureaus.

Use of In-House Computer

In past years larger professional clients were likely to use an in-house system, whereas smaller clients could not afford to do so. This is not the case today, however; smaller computers are now feasible in any size professional office.

It is true that a smaller practice does not have the need for a computer that a larger office has. Most organizations of considerable size can ill afford to be without a data processing system, whether it be an in-house or outside system. A larger practice, however, will probably be in a better position to justify the cost of an in-house system.

One question to be resolved in connection with an in-house system is whether to buy or lease. This must be decided on the same basis as any lease or buy decision:

- The long-term financial effect.
- The effect on cash flow.
- The attractiveness of terms.
- How long the equipment will be used, and the difficulty of disposing of it in case of need to change.

Another consideration with in-house equipment is the need to employ a data processing staff. The client with an in-house system assumes the costs, problems, and risks of the entire operation, including personnel and equipment acquisition.

The advantages of an in-house system, of course, are the availablity of the equipment at all times and the ability to design systems specifically to suit the client's own requirements. As the organization grows and its information needs expand, the advantages of an in-house system become more apparent.

An in-house system should be installed only after the most careful evaluation and planning. A systems analysis is required to determine both the present and future level of transactions, as well as reporting requirements. Representatives of equipment manufacturers can assist in this analysis, but the accountant should carefully review their findings, as noted earlier in this chapter.

In some cases it may be advisable to call in a consultant with data processing expertise. This is true particularly if the accountant's personal knowledge is limited.

An important point: assisting the client in selection of a data processing system is a very responsible task. The accountant with limited data processing knowledge should tread warily in this area. Don't try to do work for which you are not qualified. Call in an expert if necessary. Failure to do so could result in a poorly done system job, to the detriment of the client—and of the accountant.

Use of Smaller Computer in Professional Office

Our firm has a client operating a veterinary practice with two doctors. They use a small computer with a program designed specifically for veterinarians. While the computer is not used in connection with preparation of general accounting records, it provides information and controls that greatly enhance their operations.

Some of the data generated by the system are listed below.

- An animal record includes date, owner, list of procedures performed, drugs used and remarks as to diagnosis, symptoms, and test results.
- Charges for procedures done and drugs used are calculated.
- Monthly statements are prepared, including addition of service charges on past-due accounts.
- A running inventory of drugs is maintained, with drugs used automatically deducted from inventory.
- A complete listing of clients and names of animals can be prepared.
- A reminder schedule of shots can be prepared.
- An itemized receipt can be printed for any owner who wants one.
- Year-to-date income generated by each type of treatment can be reported.
- Income generated by each doctor can be identified by using a doctor number on each service rendered.
- A daily receipts report can be prepared.

The client has stated that before they obtained the computer they used an antiquated billing system that was totally lacking in control. Upon converting to the computer they found unbilled charges and uncollected accounts of which they were unaware. It is their belief that the computer will pay for itself through better billing and collection practices.

Use of Service Bureaus

In many cases sending the data processing out to a service bureau is deemed a better choice than acquiring in-house equipment. This is particularly true where the data processing needs are such that a service bureau can fill them readily.

Some service bureaus specialize in one type of industry or profession. They provide well-designed programs and reports at a reasonable cost. The client who has this type of service available should take advantage of it if it meets his needs.

The service bureau should be checked out. Timeliness, reliability, and cost are important criteria. Location is a factor, although it is not unusual to find satisfied customers who use bureaus far away from home.

The service bureau's programs and reports should be reviewed carefully as to whether they serve the client's needs. Determine whether the programs are flexible, or whether there are alternatives from which to choose. Inquire about the procedure to be followed for correcting errors.

Ask whether there is a "trial run" period during which the results can be checked out. Further, be sure that the first month's results are closely monitored. The client should maintain his old system on a parallel basis until fully satisfied with the reliability of the product.

Use of On-Line Equipment

A more sophisticated approach to data processing service, and one with a considerable following among professionals, is use of on-line equipment. The client has direct access to a computer in a remote location, transmitting data on an immediate access basis, generally through telephone lines.

Some of the advantages of on-line equipment:

- Access to large sophisticated equipment without the problems of ownership.
- Ability to transmit and receive data immediately.
- Ability to keep all necessary data up-to-date on a daily basis. This applies not only to financial data, but to such items as patients' records, etc.

Some of the disadvantages:

- The cost.
- Occasional unreliability of transmission through telephone lines.
- Need to train people to operate the equipment in the client's office (which is not required in case of a straight service bureau system).

All the points made regarding checking out a service bureau apply to an on-line operation. Teamwork is even more important here because the client's personnel are working directly with bureau personnel. The client's personnel have responsibility for input, so errors can occur at either end. A clear understanding and good working relationship are very important.

With an on-line system the client can receive data visually on a screen or in printed form, or both. The client will have to decide whether he wants all reports, statements, etc. printed out in his office, or whether the printouts can be prepared in the computer center. In the latter case the client can use a CRT display screen to call up information he needs. The cost, of course, increases as features are added to the system.

A well-designed on-line system that is working smoothly can be a valuable asset to the client's operation. In fact, he will probably wonder how he got along without it. Achieving these results, however, takes patience and a willingness to learn the system and adapt to it. Some clients may not be able to make this change. For those who can, the results will be well worth it.

Using the Accountant's Data Processing Service

The preceding discussions have assumed the use of a service bureau not connected with the accountant's office. A data processing alternative is for the accountant himself to provide the service. Many accounting firms have computers, offer a variety of data processing services for clients, and can offer advantages over the service bureau route.

The accountant has the advantage of prior knowledge of the client's system and problems in general. He already has a relationship with the client. He is prepared to render a complete professional service, rather than merely operating a computer. He is in a position, therefore, to serve the client's needs effectively, and may very likely provide the best service.

The accountant probably is located in the same community as the client and can avoid problems that arise from long distance processing with out-of-town service bureaus.

Some specialized bureaus have programs the accountant may not be able to match. In this event an objective evaluation should be made of the benefits to the client from this service. Our firm provides computer service to many clients, but we have several who use bureaus specializing in their particular industry, with programs we cannot match. In such cases, we advise the client to use the other service.

Remember the Human Factor

One of our clients has developed a highly profitable and fairly large business. He understands accounting records and knows how to use them. His general ledgers are on a manual system. He uses a mechanical calculator that is twenty years old. He continues to use this antiquated system and equipment most effectively. He refuses to change to something he doesn't understand.

This example illustrates the need to remember the human factor when dealing with accounting systems. If a client prefers a system because it works for him, be cautious in trying to make a change. Point out the advantages of modern technology, but don't push him into something he doesn't want.

With some professional clients the biggest problem may be to get their attention. Professional people are not necessarily business oriented (the lawyer client may be preoccupied with trial work, the architect may be strictly the creative type). The accountant may have to use both persistence and persuasion to get the clients to take time to look at the business and accounting side of their practices.

The client's personnel must be considered, also. They are familiar with the existing system, and perhaps originated some of its features. Keep this in mind when reviewing the system and commenting on its deficiencies.

It is particularly important when converting a client to a data processing system to have the support of the entire staff. If they are unhappy about changes in a system they invented, or feel threatened by the change, they can play havoc with the transition.

Tact and diplomacy are important when discussing system changes. The client's staff must be sold on the advantages of the new system: better records, faster reports, and less tedious hand posting. Their support and enthusiasm, or lack of it, can make or break a conversion. The successful practice of accounting requires human relations skills in dealing with clients and their personnel.

SPECIFIC POINTS REGARDING SYSTEMS FOR PROFESSIONALS

Professional clients in general, and members of certain professions in particular, will have specific problems that need to be addressed. These points are discussed in the following paragraphs.

Cash vs. Accrual Basis Accounting

Most professionals report on the cash basis for income tax purposes. To do otherwise is questionable, since there is no point in paying tax on income before it is collected.

There are, however, some distinct advantages to the use of the accrual method for reporting purposes. Our firm finds it helpful to determine profit on both the cash and accrual method each month. Accounts receivable are carried on our ledger and our financial statement as an asset. They are offset, both in the ledger and on the balance sheet, by a deferred income account, "Uncollected Fees." This account is credited for billings when they occur, and debited when the fee is collected and taken into income. Profit on the accrual basis is measured by using amounts billed as the income figure, whereas the cash basis profit reflects fees collected. Expenses are not accrued.

Architects and engineers can benefit from accrual method accounting in measuring job costs incurred against amounts billed. Accrual accounting may be essential to enable these professionals to bill properly. This would entail accrual of both income and costs. These items can be backed out at year end to provide for cash basis tax reporting.

Accounting for Receivables

A frequent weakness in the accounting system of small professional clients is in receivables. This accounting appears so simple it is often not properly set up or controlled. Receivables ledgers are maintained manually, without general ledger control and in unbound card or loose-leaf systems. As a result, there is a potential for considerable loss of revenue arising from misplaced records, posting errors, or employee embezzlement.

Poor receivable records usually mean poor collection efforts. Usually there is no reporting or aging of unpaid accounts.

The accountant should make a point of inquiring about the accounts receivable records of his professional clients, particularly in smaller offices. He should urge the client to utilize a system that provides for:

- General ledger control, with balancing each month.
- Aged trial balance of unpaid accounts weekly or monthly.
- Division of duties to the extent possible between handling of funds and posting of receivables.

There are many excellent systems available, both pegboard and data processing, which offer accounting and control advantages. The client should be alerted to the availability of these.

SPECIFIC POINTS REGARDING ACCOUNTING SYSTEMS FOR ATTORNEYS

Accounting for Trust Funds

The rules of the American Bar Association and most state bars make it a disciplinary offense if a lawyer fails to maintain a trust account for receipt of client funds. The trust accounting must be separate and apart from the office account of the lawyer.

Because of continuing concern about proper accounting for trust monies, many state bars are now establishing rules and regulations that prescribe minimum accounting records that must be maintained, and minimum accounting procedures, such as monthly reconciliations, that must be followed. Good business practice dictates that the lawyer maintain the records and follow the procedures prescribed.

The accountant should become familiar with the requirements of his state for his lawyer clients, and see that they are being followed. The basic ingredients for trust accounting are as follows:

- A separate checking accounting for trust funds.
- A record of receipts and disbursements.
- A client ledger clearly reflecting all transactions regarding funds of each client.
- A reconciliation each month of the client balances in the ledger against the funds on hand.
- A prohibition against using trust funds for any personal or office purpose.

A lawyer who misuses trust funds usually has disciplinary problems with his state bar and not infrequently receives adverse publicity. The accountant has a responsibility to keep his clients out of such trouble by keeping his eye on the trust fund accounting system.

Accounting for Expenses Advanced

Lawyers often advance court costs and other expenses in connection with cases in preparation for trial. Sometimes these advances run into substantial sums. The system should provide for accounting for these advances and a method of balancing the subsidiary ledger against a control.

Lawyer clients may raise the question of charging these advances off currently as expenses for tax purposes. The accountant should advise the client that these advances are in the nature of receivables and cannot be charged off unless they become uncollectible.

Accounting for Time Charged to Clients

Most attorneys have adopted the policy of keeping records of the time charged to clients and using this as a basis for billing. Some attorneys, however, use a rudimentary time-keeping system.

The accountant should introduce the client to an up-to-date time-keeping system (perhaps the accountant can use his own system as an example). Many systems are available through pegboard or data processing applications that can provide the lawyer with excellent records for billing purposes.

If a time-recording system is to operate effectively the attorney must be sold on it and be willing to discipline himself to maintain his own time. The accountant's first job may be that of convincing the attorney client of the importance of good time records.

Accounting for Work in Progress

Unbilled charges, or work in progress, can amount to a substantial item for a law office. The reasons for this:

- Some cases cannot be billed until completion. Cases that are prolonged can build up a considerable amount of unbilled charges while they are in progress.
- Some attorneys are lax in keeping their billings up to date. They become so preoccupied with their client work they ignore administrative matters.

A system for accounting and reporting for unbilled charges will help with this problem. The system could be similar to that used by the accountant. Most accounting firms use data processing for accumulating and reporting time charged to clients. This system could be adapted to attorney clients, with a monthly report on unbilled charges. This would keep the attorneys on their toes regarding billing on a timely basis.

SPECIFIC POINTS REGARDING ACCOUNTING SYSTEMS FOR DOCTORS

Controls in the Office

The importance of internal controls has been discussed in Chapter 5. A good control system applies to all professionals, but is perhaps of most importance to doctors. They are especially vulnerable to embezzlement because many doctors deal with a large number of patients and handle considerable cash receipts.

The accounting system should insure that:

- All patient visits are recorded, and that it is difficult for office personnel to deliberately omit this recording.
- The system for handling incoming cash has proper checks and balances and that cash is fully accounted for and deposited on a daily basis.
- Accounts receivable records are balanced at least monthly and a report of unpaid accounts is provided regularly to the doctor.

The accountant should recommend use of a pegboard system or data processing application whenever possible, since such systems have built-in features that require more discipline and control.

Accounting for Patient Charges

The doctor's revenue comes from patients seen and services performed. It is essential that the system provide a full record of these services, both for revenue and control purposes. A variety of systems are available for this purpose, one of which was illustrated in Exhibit 4-1. Pegboard systems work well in the smaller office and data processing systems are available for organizations of all sizes.

The accountant should see that the system adequately serves the client's needs, particularly in respect to determining that:

- All services rendered and patients seen are recorded, that there are no "lost" patients.
- The system provides for prompt billing.
- There is an adequate record of patient charges and collections that will satisfy audits by IRS or others.

Billing Third-Party Payors

In recent years more and more payments coming to doctors have been from claims filed with insurance companies or government agencies. This has created a perplexing paperwork burden. Office personnel have found themselves burdened with an ever-increasing workload of claim forms.

Companies supplying systems to the medical profession have come up with a variety of forms and systems designed to streamline third-party billing. The accountant who wants to assist his doctor clients in this area must become familiar with the systems offered by these vendors. They range from manual to pegboard to data processing systems, with numerous variations. As in any systems work, the accountant must evaluate the problem from the client's standpoint and analyze the solutions offered by various vendors.

SPECIFIC POINTS REGARDING ACCOUNTING SYSTEMS FOR DENTISTS

The accounting system of a dentist is quite similar to that of a doctor. The points made in the preceding paragraphs, therefore, regarding doctors are applicable to dentists. There are several additional points, however, to be considered.

Dental Office Equipment

Dentists have a considerable investment in equipment. Accounting for fixed assets, depreciation and investment tax credit is generally more important for dentists than for other professionals.

The accountant should see that records of dental office equipment are maintained in detail, either through fixed asset ledgers or on the depreciation schedule itself. With detailed records the proper depreciable life can be established and equipment items will be identifiable when the time comes to sell or trade.

The large investment in equipment frequently requires the dentist to obtain financing for this purpose. Detailed equipment records will facilitate the arranging of financing.

Scheduling

Dentists carry on an office practice, seeing numerous patients each day. One of the keys to a profitable operation is good scheduling. The technique of scheduling patients is an art in itself. The objectives of good scheduling are to:

- Make the most efficient use of the time of the dentist and assistants.
- See patients at their scheduled time without undue delay.
- Avoid idle periods during the day.

Some accounting firms with a heavy concentration of medical clients have learned scheduling techniques that permit them to serve their clients in this area. The accountant who wants to perform this service should obtain training and/or experience before undertaking an assignment.

Follow-up Reminders

The dentist needs a system for reminding patients of follow-up treatment needs. If the client is having a problem in this area the accountant can review available systems. Both pegboard and data processing systems offer this service.

SPECIFIC POINTS REGARDING ACCOUNTING SYSTEMS FOR ARCHITECTS

Architects have accounting requirements that are considerably different from those of other professionals. Some of the characteristics of architecture practice and the related accounting problems are described in the following paragraphs.

Objectives of the Accounting System

The system must be designed to properly record direct costs incurred in performing the service, and provide data for billing for services rendered. The accountant must ascertain the type of contractual arrangement the architect has with his clients in order that the system can be structured to yield the needed data.

Some specific objectives:

- To provide data that will enable appropriate billings under contracts with clients.
- To enable the architect to know what his job costs are on a current basis and to evaluate job performance.
- To maintain records that can be readily audited by clients should that need arise.
- To provide overall financial data so that proper financial controls can be maintained.
- To provide statistical data regarding jobs, to be used in connection with negotiations for future work.

Methods of Compensation for Architectural Services

There are several methods by which architects charge for their services, some of which differ considerably from methods used by other professionals. The most common methods are described below.

Percentage of Construction Cost Method

The traditional and most frequently used method is based on a percentage of the construction cost. This method is simple to use and understand. It protects the architect against inflation and changes in job plans, since the fee goes up along with construction costs. It has certain disadvantages, one of which is that the compensation so determined bears no sound relationship to the value of the services rendered. Also, the architect who works to hold down construction costs will receive less compensation as a result.

Multiplier of Direct Personnel Cost

With this method the architect essentially charges for time spent working on the project, similar to the method used by accountants. This method appears to be gaining popularity in the architecture profession. It is simple to use and permits a reasonable compensation based on amount of time and costs incurred. The client may be concerned, however, that he will not know what his total cost will be.

The accountant should see that his architect client is using an appropriate formula for determining his billing rate, one that recovers the direct cost of the job, plus a reasonable share of office overhead and a profit. This formula must be reviewed periodically to see that it stays up with changing conditions.

Fixed Fee Contract

This method is used occasionally when the scope of a job is clear, the program requirements are complete, and unusual contingencies are not anticipated. Under this method the client knows what his cost will be, but it is difficult for the architect to estimate precisely what his project cost will be.

The accountant should caution his client that when using this method he must exercise utmost care in estimating his costs, and should include an extra margin for contingencies. Failure to follow this cautious approach could lead to incurring a significant loss on a job.

Billing for Services Performed

The architect should arrange to bill regularly and to keep his unbilled services as low as possible. Billing arrangements must be determined at the time the contract is negotiated.

On a percentage-of-construction-cost contract the architect should have an understanding with his client as to the length of the engagement and what is to be accomplished and billed at specified periods. Time and expense records must be recorded on a current basis so that billing can be accomplished as promptly as possible. A monthly summary of applicable costs should be part of the system (see Exhibit 4-4).

Time and Expense Reporting

The accountant should insist that his architect client install an adequate system for time and expense reporting. The reporting of time can be similar to that used in the accountant's own office. The main problem may be that of getting the client himself to realize the importance of this function. As stated before, some professional men are not business or accounting oriented, are preoccupied with their own work for clients, and may be averse to record keeping. This, then, is a hurdle the accountant must face in installing the system.

Cost Accounting

Architects incur a variety of costs in connection with rendering their services:

• Professional service—time spent by the firm's personnel on the job.

- Cost of employing outside consultants and engineers.

- Other direct out-of-pocket costs, such as copying, telephone, and travel.

Out-of-pocket costs can be a significant portion of the cost of a job. These should be anticipated when negotiating a contract.

The accounting system should compare job costs incurred on a continuing basis as the job progresses. Generally a data processing system will more adequately keep this information up to date than other systems. The accountant's in-house computer may be the best method of handling this need.

General Accounting System and Financial Reports

Several points should be considered in setting up the chart of accounts and operating statement format. These points are as follows:

- Whether the system should reflect the cash or the accrual method of reporting, particularly for income and direct job costs.

- Whether to allocate overhead costs to jobs.

- Whether to report income on the operating statement based on billings rendered, or whether to report "billable work performed," providing a measurement of underbilling or overbilling.

The operating statement should reflect accrual figures for both income and direct job costs. This provides the best measure of operating results. It can be converted back to a cash basis operating statement for tax reporting purposes.

Direct job costs should be segregated and reported as such on the operating statement. This includes salaries and other costs.

The allocation of overhead to jobs is of questionable value. It is recommended that the direct job cost approach be used unless the client has a particular need or desire for such allocation.

Most clients probably do not need reporting of "billable work performed" on the operating statement. This type of reporting introduces a more complicated approach, which probably should be avoided unless there is a specific reason to use it. A less complicated operating statement will be utilized to better advantage by most clients.

The measurement of billable work against actual billings can be done as supplementary reporting without getting it into the operating statement itself. It is an important measurement which should be utilized, particularly for larger clients.

Similarity of Architects and Engineers

This discussion can be applied to engineering firms as well as to architects. Employment arrangements, types of costs incurred and methods of operations are quite similar.

SPECIFIC POINTS REGARDING ACCOUNTING SYSTEMS FOR INSURANCE AGENTS

Accounting Problems and Requirements

Insurance agents offering a wide range of coverage (casualty, property, medical, life) have certain characteristics that affect their accounting needs:

- The agent usually bills the customer, collects the premium, and remits it to the insurance company after deducting his commission.
- The agent generally handles a substantial sum of money.
- Accounts receivable are generally sizable.

Internal Controls

The handling of substantial sums requires that internal controls be adequate. The accountant should see that every effort is made to provide a division of duties between the person handling cash and the person recording it.

Accounts Receivable

A system should be in effect that provides adequate reporting and controls. Collection follow-up is essential because of the sums of money involved.

Accounting for Amounts Owed Insurance Companies

The amounts due companies should be reconciled monthly between detailed accounting records, control accounts, and general ledger accounts. Agents with good systems have been known to develop significant out-of-balance problems with company accounts. Again, substantial sums are involved and the system must provide for adequate controls. Any misstatement of company liabilities generally results in a corresponding misstatement of commission income, since the two are related.

Computerized Systems

Well-designed systems have been developed by computer service bureaus, providing comprehensive services including customer billing, general ledgers, accounts receivable ledgers, and financial statements. Many insurance agents find these services solve a lot of record-keeping problems. Such systems can get fouled up, however, and require continual monitoring by a knowledgeable person.

PLEASE RETURN THIS FORM TO THE RECEPTIONIST

2014

PREVIOUS BALANCE

PATIENT NAME

OFFICE VISIT—New Patient	CRVS/CSN	FEE
( ) Brief	90000	$
( ) Limited	90010	$
( ) Intermediate	90015	$
( ) Comprehensive	90020	$
( ) Complex	90026	$

OFFICE VISIT—Estab. Patient		
( ) Brief	90040	$
( ) Limited	90050	$
( ) Intermediate	90060	$
( ) Extended	90070	$
( ) Comprehensive	90080	$

LABORATORY		
( ) Pap Smear	88150	$
( ) VDRL	86597	$
( ) Throat Culture	87060	$
( ) SMA 12	80112	$
( ) SMA 18	80116	$
( ) 1181	80119	$
( ) Electrolytes	80104	$
( ) Thyroid Profile	80104	$
( ) CBC	85022	$
( ) Potassium	84132	$
( ) Urinalysis	81000	$
( ) Hemoglobin	83020	$
( ) Hematocrit	85014	$
( ) Sed Rate	85650	$

OTHER PROFESSIONAL SERVICES

DIAGNOSIS:

CONSULT—( ) Office ( ) Hospital	CRVS/CSN	FEE
( ) Limited	90600	$
( ) Intermediate	90605	$
( ) Extensive	90610	$
( ) Comprehensive	90620	$
( ) Complex	90025	$

CONSULT—Follow-Up—( ) Office ( ) Hospital		
( ) Brief	90640	$
( ) Limited	90641	$
( ) Intermediate	90642	$
( ) Extended	90643	$

HOSPITAL CARE—Initial Visit		
( ) Intermediate	90215	$
Date		
( ) Comprehensive	90220	$
Date		

HOSPITAL CARE—Follow-Up Visits		
( ) Brief ___ Days		
@ $ ___ per visit	90240	$
Dates		
( ) Limited ___ Days		
@ $ ___ per visit	90250	$
Dates		
( ) Intermed. ___ Days		
@ $ ___ per visit	90260	$
Dates		
( ) Extended ___ Days		
@ $ ___ per visit	90270	$
Dates		

HOSPITAL—Critical Care		
( ) Initial Visit	90290	$
Dates		
( ) Intermed Visit ___ Days		
@ $ ___ per visit	90296	$

Date of Service		

HOSPITAL—Other Visits	CRVS/CSN	FEE
( ) Detention ___ Hours		
@ $	90040	$
( ) Discharge Day	90275	$
Date		

EMERGENCY ROOM VISITS		
( ) After Hours	99042	$
( ) During Office Hours	99043	$

OTHER SERVICES		
( ) Supplies	99070	$
( ) Electrocardiogram	93000	$
( ) Rhythm Strip	93040	$
( ) Single Venipuncture & Centrifuge	99009	$
( ) Cocci Skin Test	86490	$
( ) TB Skin Test	86580	$
( ) Anoscopy	40260	$
( ) Sigmoidoscopy	40240	$
( ) Immunization	90720	$
( ) Injection	90730	$
( ) Nursing Home Visit		$

HOSPITALIZATION	
☐ DOWNEY COMMUNITY	
☐ RIO HONDO HOSPITAL	
☐	

TOTAL CHARGES $

SAFEGUARD CLINIC
6117 MALT AVENUE
LOS ANGELES, CA 90040
(213) 724-1666
IRS NO. 12-345678   PROV. NO. 87654

REFERRING PHYSICIAN

DOCTOR'S SIGNATURE:

ASSIGNMENT AND RELEASE: I hereby authorize my insurance benefits be paid directly to the physician and I am financially responsible for non-covered services. I also authorize the physician to release any information required in the processing of this claim.

Signed _____ Date _____

NOTICE TO INSURANCE CARRIERS: This form has been devised to reduce costs. If any additional forms or itemized bills are required they will be completed upon the receipt of $25.00.

( ) I Do/Do Not Accept Assignment   ( ) Date Symptoms Appeared or Accident Occurred _____

RETURN: ___ Days ___ Weeks ___ Months   NEXT APPT. _____

Form No. QC-M11-WD   1/80   10152

Form courtesy of Safeguard Business Systems, Inc.

Exhibit 4-1: Client or Patient Billings

Vincent Mathews vs. _____ All Coverage Ins. _____

CASE OR FILE NO. #1701

R.A. Healy

DATE	NAME	MEMO	TRUST FUNDS RECEIVED	TRUST FUNDS DISBURSED	COSTS RECOVERED	COSTS ADVANCED	DATE BILLED	CK.-REC. CASE NO.	FEES RECEIVED	FEES CHARGED	FEE BALANCE	TRUST BALANCE	COSTS ADVANCED BALANCE
2/4	Vincent Mathews		50.00				1	#1701				50.00	
2/18	Crest Photo Service			40.00			2	2501				10.00	
4/3	County Court Clerk	Filing fee		8.50			3	3005				1.50	
4/3	City Bank & Trust Co.	Loan Repayment-V. Matthews				785.00	4	2099					785.00
4/3	City Hospital	Phy. Exam-V. Matthews				35.00	5	3000					820.00
4/4	All Coverage Ins.	Matthews Settlement	10,000.00				6	#1701				10,001.50	
4/4	Nealy & Myers	Cost/Fees		3,320.00			7	3023		2,500.00	2,500.00	6,681.50	
4/4	Vincent Mathews-Transfer (3,320.00)				820.00		8	#1701	2,500.00		-0-		-0-
4/5	Vincent Mathews	Final Settlement		6,681.50			9	3024				-0-	

BALANCES FORWARDED

TRUST BALANCE · FEE BALANCE · COSTS ADVANCED BALANCE

Chronological listing of all parties representing the financial transactions affecting this case

Record of all deposits and disbursements affecting the client's trust account

Provides client misc. charges and cost advanced information

All entries on this ledger are created as a result of checks disbursed from general and trust bank accounts; all cash received and fees charged entries are made on one of three self-balancing journals that assure accuracy and control.

Record of fees charged and received

Client's current balance

CLIENTS LEDGER

Form courtesy of Safeguard Business Systems, Inc.

Exhibit 4-2: Accounting for Trust Funds

NEW MATTER REPORT

CLIENT INFORMATION

CLIENT: _____ Date _____ 19 ____

ADDRESS: _____ ◯ NEW CLIENT ◯ PRESENT CLIENT

_____ SOC. SEC. # _____ / ____ / ____
(City)   (Code)

BUSINESS PHONE: _____ CLIENT NUMBER _____

CONTACT: _____ HOME PHONE: _____

MATTER INFORMATION

FILE NAME: _____

NATURE OF MATTER: _____

_____

_____

_____

AMOUNT INVOLVED: _____ AREA OF PRACTICE CODE: _____

OPPOSING PARTY: _____
                          Name   Address   Phone No.

_____

OPPOSING LAWYER: _____
                          Name   Address   Phone No.

FEE ARRANGEMENT

◯ FIXED FEE OF $ _____ OR RANGE OF $ _____ TO $ _____

◯ TIME RATE _____

◯ CONTINGENCY OF: _____

◯ FEE TO BE DETERMINED ON BASIS OF WORK DONE, TAKING INTO ACCOUNT ALL RELEVANT FACTORS.

◯ OTHER: _____ | CLIENT SIGNATURE

ESTIMATED FEE $ _____ |

BILLING PROCEDURE

◯ NEW GENERAL RETAINER $ _____ PER _____ EFFECTIVE _____

◯ OPENING ADVANCE OF $ _____

◯ BILLING INSTRUCTIONS FOR BOOKKEEPER:

	MONTHLY	QUARTERLY	UPON CONCLUSION	OTHER
FEE	◯	◯	◯	◯
DISBURSEMENTS	◯	◯	◯	◯

OTHER: _____

FILES

FILE CARDS PREPARED BY: _____ DATE _____

◯ OPEN NEW FILE   ◯ INCLUDE IN EXISTING FILE   ◯ NO FILE

FILES CHECKED FOR CONFLICT OF INTEREST BY: _____ DATE _____

FIRM ADMINISTRATION

OPENED BY _____ ENGAGEMENT RECEIVED FROM _____

RESPONSIBLE LAWYER _____ ENGAGEMENT RECEIVED BY _____

ASSIGNED LAWYERS _____

COMMENTS _____

REMARKS

_____

_____

STATUTE OF LIMITATIONS DATE |

FORM NO. NMR-2 (74S)

Safeguard
BUSINESS SYSTEMS, INC.

ORDER FROM YOUR LOCAL SAFEGUARD DISTRIBUTOR. IF UNKNOWN, CALL 800-523-2422. IN PA. CALL 215-699-3544 COLLECT.

Form courtesy of Safeguard Business Systems, Inc.   **Exhibit 4-3: New Matter Report**

ARCHITECTS JOB COST REPORT

EAST LAKE PLAZA

MONTH ENDING MARCH 31

	HOURS		BILLING VALUE	
	Current Month	Job to Date	Current Month	Job to Date
Architectural Services				
Schematic Design				
Nelson	6	42	270	1890
Harris	108	305	3240	9150
Phillips	20	76	400	1520
	134	423	3910	12560
Design Development				
Nelson	4	36	180	1620
Harris	60	205	1800	6150
Phillips	140	190	2800	3800
	204	431	4780	11570
Total Architectural	338	854	8690	24130
Consultants				
Mech. & Elect.			4000	5500
Structural			400	850
Landscaping			5000	7500
Other Reimbursables				
Travel			150	430
Reproduction			80	200
Total Consultants and Reimbursables			9630	14480
Total Billable Amount			18320	38610

PREPARED BY   DATE

Kraftbilt BOX 800 TULSA OK 74101 5003 IVORY; 5203 GREEN; 5403 WHITE   PRINTED IN U.S.A.

Exhibit 4-4: Architect's Job Cost Report

Audits and Reviews for Professionals—Why, When and How

NEED FOR AUDITS BY PROFESSIONAL CLIENTS

More Need Than Is Generally Realized

Most accountants feel that professional clients provide a limited market for audit work. The need for audits by professionals is normally infrequent, and not much audit work is done unless the accountant is especially adept at pointing out the advantages of this service.

While it is true that there is limited need for audited financial statements by professional clients, there are many benefits that stem from an audit. Further, special audits of limited scope can be performed to meet a specific need. The accountant who wants to do this work should put some time and effort into thinking about the needs of his clients and how he can meet them. With some imagination and salesmanship he can develop a market where none existed.

This chapter will provide pointers for discovering the need for audit work, will give guidance on the performance of the work, will discuss special audit opportunities, and will consider when a "reviewed" financial statement should be issued.

Some Benefits of an Audit

A client who is considering spending money for audit service must be able to see where the benefits justify the cost. Audit service is generally discretionary; the client isn't required to buy it, so he wants to see the benefit. Here are some advantages that can be pointed out:

- An audit keeps the client's personnel (including the client) on their toes.
- An audit provides an opportunity to point out loose procedures and wasteful practices.
- An audit frequently results in recommendations that save the client time and money.
- An audit usually brings recommendations that strengthen the client's controls.
- If the client is providing financial statements to outsiders, the audit lends credibility.
- An audit is a plus factor in case of an IRS examination.

Audit of Larger Professional Clients

Professional organizations continue to grow larger as the needs for legal, engineering, medical, and other professional services increase; the larger the organization, the more need there is for an audit. A larger organization will have several owners, and an audit is an excellent tool for helping maintain good relations among them by providing assurance that their accounting and financial affairs are in order.

In a larger professional organization there will be a distinct line between those members engaged in management activities and those engaged in practice activities. The practice-oriented members are not involved in management or financial aspects of the organization and are relying on others. An audit will give assurance to practice members, while at the same time helping management discharge its responsibilities.

Larger organizations have more capital requirements and are more likely to be borrowing money. An audit will be of assistance in dealing with the lender.

Larger orgnaizations have an office and accounting staff on which the members rely to handle the money and maintain the accounting records. Accounting controls become more important and the audit will provide an outside, objective look at these controls.

The larger professional organization has the same potential benefits from an audit as does a commercial client; diversified ownership, management separated at least to some extent from ownership, capital requirements, and need for controls. The accountant for such an organization should, therefore, give serious consideration to pointing out the benefits and recommending an audit.

Don't Overlook the Smaller Client

It's easy to write off the smaller client as having little or no audit potential. Don't do that. Any successful client (and most professionals are successful) has potential for some type of audit service. The beneifts outlined above apply equally to smaller clients, and can be of significant importance to them. The smaller client is likely to be very busy in the practice of his profession, and neglecting the management side of the practice. Many professionals don't like management problems and prefer to delegate them to someone else. They will frequently turn all financial and accounting matters over to an office manager or assistant, who may or may not be capable and who may or may not be trustworthy. Certainly a client operating in this environment can use a service that examines his financial controls and accounting records.

Some of the services that can help the smaller client are discussed later in this chapter under "Special Audit Situations."

Embezzlements in Professional Offices

There is a widespread concern among accountants who deal with professional clients that such clients, particularly doctors, are more susceptible to embezzlement than commercial clients. This concern has a great deal of validity. There is no way of knowing the extent of such embezzlements. Professional men are jealous of their reputations and usually reluctant to report that they have been taken by an embezzler. The embezzlement, therefore, goes unreported.

The situation, particularly in a smaller doctor's office, is ideal for an embezzler. Here are some of the ingredients:

1. The client is busy with professional duties and prefers not to be involved with day-to-day office management matters.
2. There is little, if any, division of duties.
3. Revenue comes from many different sources, sometimes in small amounts and in cash.
4. Accounting controls, such as balancing deposits with daily receipts and balancing patients ledgers, do not exist or are disregarded due to press of other duties.
5. Check signing is delegated by the professional to an office employee.
6. There is no awareness of such controls as mandatory annual vacations.

The accountant must be alert to these situations and talk to the client. Provide him with one or more lists of danger signals regarding employee dishonesty (see Exhibit 5-1). Discuss steps that can be taken to strengthen controls, and describe audit procedures that will help avert or discover an embezzlement.

In such discussions with the client avoid giving a guarantee that an audit will catch any and all embezzlements. Many clients have a misconception about this, thinking an audit provides full assurance against employee dishonesty. Emphasize that an audit *might* catch an embezzlement, but more important, could go a long way toward heading one off by removing employee temptation.

No accountant wants to be in a situation of having a client who has discovered an embezzlement. Any time the community learns of an embezzlement the question inevitably arises as to who the accountant is. His image can be tarnished even though he has never done any work on the client's system or controls and has absolutely no responsibility.

The accountant's own self-interest, therefore, is served by getting involved in this area. He should strive to see that his professional clients are as embezzlement-proof as possible. This is part of his responsibility, it is good service, it will probably save him from embarrassing situations, and will make for a better and more appreciative client.

PERFORMANCE OF THE AUDIT WORK

Reaching an Understanding with the Client

A clear understanding with the client is imperative before undertaking any audit work. When performing an audit for the first time obtain an engagement letter. The letter should clearly state the nature and scope of the work to be performed and the fee arrangement.

As stated above, there should be a full discussion with the client of the nature of the audit and its purpose. Particularly, the client should be advised that a normal audit is for the purpose of expressing an opinion on financial statements and is not designed to discover embezzlements, although it frequently does so, and undoubedtly prevents many more. Even though this language is covered in the engagement letter, it should be discussed verbally.

Need for Top Quality Performance

Top quality performance is necessary in all phases of the accountant's work. Only by doing a first class job can he command the respect and confidence of clients, which is the basis for building a growing practice. Indeed, the one mistake that can do the most damage to the accountant's reputation is to do poor work.

All these points can be made concerning audit work, and with special emphasis:

1. The examination of, and reporting on, financial statements is the one professional service reserved exclusively for the accountant.

2. The profession has well-defined standards and abundant literature explaining the auditor's responsibilities.

3. An error, either of omission or commission, discovered after the completion of audit work is especially embarrassing.

This is a good time to stress the need for adequate liability insurance. Any work performed by the accountant is subject to potential lawsuits if errors are found and other parties damaged. Audit work probably has more potential liability hazard than other types of work. Third parties who lose money because of placing reliance on audited financial statements frequently sue the accountant for recovery of damages. Liability insurance, then, along with a program of quality control that assures first class work, are the methods used by the accountant to protect himself.

Doing the Job at a Reasonable Cost

The accountant who wants to sell audit work to professional clients must be conscious of the cost; cost is a prime factor in whether the client will decide to have the work done. There are two approaches to making the fee acceptable; make the audit so useful the client will feel it is well worth the price, and use all the time-saving techniques you can.

One approach to saving time is to have the client prepare as much material as possible. The client's personnel might be able to prepare various schedules, analyses, and the trial balance. It is best to review in advance what can be done in this area and reach an understanding in writing with the client.

One word of caution: don't let the client's personnel do work that is part of the audit itself. Select with care the work they are to do, and then carefully check and verify their work.

Here is a list of points that you can make with a client on ways to make the audit go more efficiently:

1. Provide adequate, reasonably private working space for the auditors.

2. Client's personnel should spend some time with the auditor reviewing the prior audit and planning this one.

3. Keep you advised in advance of unusual or significant transactions so the accounting matters can be resolved currently.

4. Assist in preparing schedules requested by you.

5. Have supporting data available without a time-consuming search.

6. Discuss the use of their data processing system for preparation of certain analyses.

7. Ask the client to pave the way for smooth relations with his staff.

Review of Internal Control

A review of internal control is one of the procedures required by professional literature in the conduct of an audit. It is, in fact, a most important step—one that will highlight weaknesses in the system of accounting controls, resulting in recommendations to strengthen these weaknesses. This is one of the major benefits of an audit.

Many professional organizations are small, which could lead to the conclusion that there is little opportunity for internal control. Every client, no matter how small, has inherent characteristics that can be developed into an effective system of controls. The accountant's job is to educate the client to utilize the strengths that are present. Internal control not only involves safeguards to minimize errors and reduce the risk of fraud, but also emphasizes a clear definition of duties and responsibilities, proper utilization of personnel and the system of accounting and reporting. In a small organization the owner must be vitally interested and take an active part in the system of internal control.

The cost of the audit is directly affected by the effectiveness of internal control. Without adequate internal control a more detailed examination must be made, increasing the time and cost involved. Testing and sampling can be used more effectively when good controls are in place.

One of the problems encountered in the small professional office is that of setting up an appropriate division of duties, which is a cornerstone of any control system. An office staff of one person hardly lends itself to an effective division of duties. Offsetting this, however, is something better: an alert and interested owner. The smaller the business, the more control is usually exercised by the owner. If the owner is inclined to assume certain responsibilities the accountant can utilize his or efforts most effectively.

Some professional clients may not have the time or inclination for tasks that effectuate better control. The accountant must evaluate the situation and react accordingly. Some clients might be reluctant, but would agree to certain responsibilities if the accountant sells them on the importance of it. Some clients might not want to offend long-term employees, while others might feel that a system of controls is only for a large organization. The client should be made aware of the importance of controls and the vital role he or she can play.

The review of internal control should be conducted at the beginning of the audit. It is here that information is gathered and decisions made on the extent to which auditing tests will be required. Internal control review performed toward the end of the audit is much less effective than that done at the beginning.

Internal control questionnaires are an important part of this review. Most firms have such questionnaires, some of which are designed for the smaller organization. An example of one such questionnaire is found in Exhibit 5-2, and could readily be adapted to use with professional clients.

The accountant also must keep in mind the basic elements of a good system of internal control. A list of these elements is provided in Exhibit 5-3. While not every point on the list can be utilized with each client, a handy reference list is useful as a reminder of basic elements to be kept in mind.

SPECIAL AUDIT SITUATIONS

The need for audit work on the part of professional clients need not be limited to the performance of a full audit. An audit leading to an opinion on the financial statements may not be what the client needs. A service covering audit work in specific areas may be more useful. Members of different professions have differing problems and needs, and the opportunities to perform such services may be varied. For example:

- Medical practitioners, who are considered vulnerable to embezzlement, could benefit from auditing procedures covering cash and receivable transactions.

- Lawyers occasionally get into difficulty because of careless or improper handling of trust funds, so an audit of this part of their practice might be in order.

Review of Office Procedures and Controls

A specific type of audit engagment that would be useful to any client is an examination of his office procedures and controls. There are two objectives to such an examination:

- Evaluation of the efficiency of the office.
- Evaluation of the effectiveness of the control system.

Chapter 2 discusses the need for an efficient office and the many elements making up an efficient operation. This chapter should be reviewed prior to undertaking such an engagement.

An engagement regarding the effectiveness of controls should be approached along the lines of a review of internal control. The engagement should go deeper than an internal review for audit purposes, however. The specific purpose of the engagement is to review the control system and all facets of office controls should be examined.

The engagement should have a written program outlining the scope of the work and the steps to be taken. There should be a preliminary review of the client's office before writing the program to get an idea of the problems to be encountered.

The work should be performed so that the entire review is made within a short period of time, giving the accountant an uninterrupted picture of the situation. For most professional clients this should not be difficult. Concentrate totally on the job at hand—avoid getting sidetracked on discussions of income tax problems and other matters. The engagement will produce better results if it is performed and completed promptly.

The final result of the engagement should be a written report to the client outlining the findings and recommendations. The client will attach more importance to written recommendations than to those made orally.

Limited Audits of Selected Areas

The preceding paragraphs discussed some instances where auditing of selected areas would be beneficial to the professional client. Certain audit procedures that could be applied are discussed below.

Audit of Cash Receipts of a Medical Practitioner. A simple way for an employee to embezzle from a doctor is to hold back a patient's check (for $100.00, for example). The patient's ledger card is credited but the check is not deposited or entered in the cash receipts records. The next time $100.00 in cash is received from a patient the employee pockets the cash and deposits the check to cover the receipt given for the cash, at the same time crediting the patient who paid cash. The cash receipts records agree with bank deposits, but the credits to patient's ledger cards are $100.00 in excess of cash deposited.

The employee stealing in this manner is probably doing it regularly. It is likely that a spot check of one or two months will catch the discrepancy. The accountant should run totals on three separate items:

1. Amounts deposited.
2. Cash received per cash receipts records.
3. Credits to patient's ledger accounts.

An embezzlement scheme of this type can be uncovered by relatively simple audit steps.

Audits of Receivables. An audit of cash receipts should generally be accompanied by an audit of receivables. The steps to be taken should be along these lines:

1. Confirm with negative confirmations all accounts receivable.
2. Check accounts receivable total from tape of cards to the control balance.
3. Test check the accounts receivable tape to the accounts receivable ledger cards.
4. Test check charge tickets for _____ weeks. Trace from charge tickets to accounts receivable cards.
   a. List any cards for charges that cannot be found.
   b. Account for all prenumbered charge tickets in test week.
5. Test check credits to account receivable cards.
   a. See that all noncash credits are approved by client.
   b. Trace from ledger card to daily cash receipts.
   c. Trace from the daily cash receipts to the ledger card.
   d. Trace daily receipts to bank statements from _____ to _____.

PROVIDING A "REVIEW" SERVICE

There will be occasions when the professional client requires a financial statement in connection with a proposed loan, but doesn't need an audited statement. In this situation the accountant and the client must consider which type of financial statement to use.

Distinction Between "Reviewed" and "Compiled" Financial Statements

In recent years the accounting profession has developed new types of services in connection with presentation of unaudited financial statements. Whereas previously all unaudited statements were issued with a disclaimer that they were unaudited and the accountant could express no opinion, now two levels of unaudited statements are available; compiled statements and reviewed statements.

A compiled statement is presented in a situation where the accountant's primary function is the assembling of data in financial statement form, without any significant review of the data itself. The accountant's report to the reader of the statement says he or she offers no opinion or other form of assurance regarding it.

A reviewed statement falls between audited and compiled statements. Certain inquiries and analytical procedures are performed, after which the accountant offers limited assurance by stating that he or she is not aware of any material modifications needed for the statements to conform with generally accepted accounting principles.

Advantages of a "Review" Service

The development of compiled and reviewed statements affords the accountant an opportunity to offer a service more flexible than the choice of "audited" or "unaudited." By performing a review service, he can offer certain assurances regarding the statements. In many cases the reader will find that a reviewed statement satisfies his needs, thus saving the client the added expense of an audit. The accountant should be familiar with this service and offer it when appropriate.

The practitioner will have to determine to what extent he is willing to provide clients with compiled statements for outside use. Compiled statements are appropriate for interim reporting to management, but leave something to be desired for outside use. The accountant's denial of any form of assurance on the statement can reflect on both the accountant and the client in the eyes of the reader. The accountant would be well advised, therefore, to limit the outside use of compiled statements; try to persuade the client to authorize a review service.

A review service not only improves outside reporting, it is a useful service to the client in several respects. The review procedures require, for example, checking of bank reconciliations, seeing that accounts receivable subsidiaries are in balance with controls, and the like. The performance of these procedures keeps the client's personnel on their toes.

A review service requires that the accountant look into inventories, accruals, liabilities and other accounting matters. The end result of this is a better quality financial statement. Indeed, the accountant would perform many of these steps even if he or she were not doing a review service. In most cases the review service represents a limited extension of work that would be done in any event to be sure the financial statement was in order. The performance of the review service should encompass certain specific steps, which are discussed in the order of their accomplishment.

Discuss with Client. The discussion with the client should cover the following points:

- Advantages of a review service.

- What the client needs in the way of financial statements for outside use; the type of outside users and the reasons they need the statements.

- Any weaknesses the client perceives in the accounting system and how a review service could help.

These discussions should conclude with a decision by the client as to what type of service he or she will authorize.

Obtain Engagement Letter. After the client has authorized the work an engagement letter should be obtained.

Perform the Review Work. The performance of the work should be accomplished in a systematic manner so that all necessary steps are undertaken. It is essential that a check list be followed to insure a complete approach. The check list used by our firm is found in Exhibit 5-4.

Draft Financial Statements and Report. Be sure the statements represent full disclosure and are in accordance with current reporting standards. Look the statements over with a critical eye to determine if they communicate effectively.

Obtain a Representation Letter. A representation letter is not a required step in connection with reviewed statements, but it is a recommended one. The accountant would be well advised to make a practice of obtaining a representation letter with each review engagement.

Review the Report with the Client. When the report has been completed it should be reviewed carefully with the client. This is one of the most important parts of the job. It is essential that the accountant communicate effectively with the client regarding the financial statements. Failure to do so could reduce the impact of an otherwise first-class professional job.

The final section of this chapter discusses the importance of effective communication and provides pointers for the accountant. In connection with any financial statement, whether it be audited, reviewed or compiled, keep these principles in mind:

- The client doesn't always understand figures and accounting terminology.

- The client deserves a full explanation and review of the financial statements.

- The accountant who can communicate will be more effective with the clients.

- Don't become so busy that you fail to take time to communicate with clients.

REPORTING FINANCIAL DATA AND AUDIT RESULTS

Effective Communication—an Essential Tool

An accountant spends much of his or her time communicating; speaking, listening, writing, reading, and is in continual contact with clients, attorneys, bankers, IRS personnel, and others. The effectiveness of the accountant's professional work is strongly linked to the ability to communicate.

The accountant's objective is to convey useful facts and advice; this is what clients are paying for. The client who can't understand the accountant because of poor communication won't be an enthusiastic client.

Keep the word "useful" in mind. Clients don't want to pay for a report or advice that is not useful. A financial statement is not useful if the client can't understand it. The accountant deals in a technical, complex field with its own terminology that isn't easily understood by others. Words and ideas must be readily understood; it is the accountant who must determine what facts and advice will be most useful to the client.

When you communicate effectively and convey useful information you are selling yourself. This is a significant byproduct of good communication. Selling yourself is necessary in the building of an accounting practice, and nothing helps more than effective, useful communication.

Communicating Financial Data. Professional clients vary greatly in the type and complexity of financial data required. The size of the professional practice, as well as the type of professional activity, will influence and dictate the financial reporting. The accountant must be adaptable in handling the varied types of reporting and communicating situations that are presented. There are, however, certain basic types of information that should be communicated in all cases. In determining what to communicate to the client, the accountant should attempt to put himself or herself into the client's position; what information does that client want and need? Here are some points to keep in mind.

Analyzing the Operating Results. Give the client some guidelines against which to measure results. Income and expense categories can be measured against several yardsticks:

- Prior year's figures.
- The budget, if one was prepared.
- Statistics reflecting averages in the profession.

Be sure to note any trends you detect in reviewing the figures. Use percentages, ratios, and five-years' trends to help communicate.

Reporting on Financial Condition. The balance sheet should be prepared in comparative form. Ratios and percentages should again be used to analyze and highlight important items. A summary of assets and liabilities over a five-year period can be useful.

Reporting on Where the Profit Went. One of the most common problems encountered by an accountant is the inability of clients to understand where their funds went. A statement of changes in financial position will normally help provide answers, but more may be required for the professional client. If substantial amounts have been withdrawn from the practice and used for investments or personal purposes it may be necessary to highlight this information.

Looking to the Future. When discussing financial statements, be alert to any client comments about future plans. This could provide an opportunity to analyze future commitments or provide projections and budgets. A budgeting program for the professional practice, as described in Chapter 3, is a very useful service. The accountant who works with a client in this context sheds the image of being only a recorder of past history and becomes a management adviser.

Use of Charts. Some people understand charts better than columns of figures. The accountant should develop skills in presenting information in this manner and be in a position to use it when appropriate.

Learn to Express Yourself Clearly. If you will make an extra effort to work on your communication skills you will find the time well spent. Review your written reports with a critical eye; work them over to make them more understandable. Practice verbal communication so that it is effective.

The Management Letter. The management letter is a widely used method of communication, commenting on a wide range of matters observed during the audit. Management letters can be made more effective by following some of the following basic principles.

Avoid enumerating minor discrepancies in the books. Normally the client isn't particularly interested in such items, and it detracts from other important comments.

Be sure the letter is well organized. If the letter covers a variety of topics, break it down into categories. Comments regarding accounting matters, for example, should be separated from those regarding internal control, office procedures, general management comments, and the like. In some instances the letter might have comments that should be passed along to different people, and can be organized to facilitate this distribution.

Sometimes recommendations must be made that the client does not care to follow. Recommendations regarding weaknesses in internal control are a necessary part of the letter. Even though the client cannot follow the recommendation, the auditor should make it in order to go on record concerning the problem. See Exhibit 5-5 for an example of a management letter to a professional client.

CONCLUSION

Don't overlook opportunities to perform audit work for professional clients. Become adept at recognizing the need and convincing the client of the benefit of the service. The accountant who develops this area of service will have something to offer that most accountants overlook—and will profit from it.

The following are early behavioral warning signs that may or may not be linked to an actual embezzlement. Take notice if your client's bookkeeper, receptionist, or office manager—whoever handles the money in the office—figuratively waves one or more of these alert flags.

1. Openly resents a substantial income and upper-middle-class lifestyle to the point where continual snide comments are made about it.

2. Regularly carries a lot of cash, sometimes blatantly acting as the office's resident "bank teller," cashing colleagues' checks out of a pocket "bank drawer."

3. Is casual about observing office procedures, for example, in the case of a medical office receptionist "forgetting" to post the pegboard across after doing the vertical computation; or "running out of gas" before completing the daily verification of accounts receivable.

4. Adamantly resists any change in the present accounting system, especially if the change involves the replacement of an antiquated system with an easier, more efficient modern one.

5. Starts using new vendors for no apparent reason.

6. Is overzealous about collecting on overdue accounts, using high-pressure telephone solicitation techniques that never seem to bring results.

7. Produces sloppy records that have a lot of erasures and are hard to decipher.

8. Is lax about the petty cash fund, keeping it well-stocked with IOU's from colleagues who require some cash "to tide me over 'til Monday."

9. Refuses to take vacations that last longer than two days.

10. Appears to be a workhorse who is willing—and indeed wants—to take work home or arrive before everyone else and stay late because "I work better when I'm alone."

11. Acts like an empire-builder, craving increasing amounts of responsibility and rejecting all offers of help from colleagues.

12. Seems overwrought about family or personal problems, which could include separation, divorce, or spouse who is an alcoholic, drug addict, or gambler—all problems that create severe financial pressures.

13. Abruptly changes spending patterns, purchasing big-ticket items that appear to be beyond his or her means.

14. Asks for frequent pay advances, indicating poor budgeting of personal funds, creating cash-flow problems.

Exhibit 5-1: Warning Signs of Employee Embezzlement

A. INTERNAL CONTROLS RELATED TO
BUDGET:

	Yes	No	Explain
1. Does the client prepare a budget for:			
a. Capital acquisitions?	_____	_____	_____
b. Operating income and expenses?	_____	_____	_____
c. At least yearly?	_____	_____	_____
2. Does the client periodically review the statement? Budget?	_____	_____	_____
3. Receivables management:	_____	_____	_____
a. Are accounts receivables aged?	_____	_____	_____
1) If so, how often?	_____	_____	_____
2) Is the aging format adequate?	_____	_____	_____
b. Is a delinquency report prepared?	_____	_____	_____
c. Is a schedule of insurance claims outstanding maintained by medical clients?	_____	_____	_____
d. Is payment requested at time service is rendered?	_____	_____	_____
e. Is a collection ratio prepared on a monthly basis?	_____	_____	_____
f. How long after services are rendered do billings go out?	_____	_____	_____
g. How are collection procedures handled?	_____	_____	_____
h. Does the client use a collection agency?	_____	_____	_____

B. INTERNAL CONTROLS RELATED TO PERSONNEL:

	Yes	No	Explain
1. Are all employees having access to cash bonded?	_____	_____	_____

Exhibit 5-2: Internal Control Checklist—Professional Clients

	Yes	No	Explain

2. Are employees required to take vacations?

3. Are all prospective employees carefully screened and selected:

   a. Interviewed by the client?

   b. References checked, personal and credit?

   c. Work background reviewed?

C. INTERNAL CONTROLS RELATED TO CASH:

1. Is cash handling clearly assigned to one person?

2. If receipts are written for all money received:

   a. Are serially numbered receipt slips used in numerical order?

   b. Is a copy of the receipt given to the client at the time service is performed or upon payment?

   c. Is the accounts receivable ledger card photocopied and used for billing?

   d. Is segregation of duties achieved or, if not possible, are sound cash receipts practices adhered to?

3. Are cash receipts deposited intact daily or, if not possible, is the deposit slip prepared before closing and a duplicate deposit slip prepared and safeguarded?

4. Has the bank been instructed in writing not to cash checks made payable to the client?

5. Are NSF checks returned directly to the client and then reentered on the books?

Exhibit 5-2: Internal Control Checklist—Professional Clients (Continued)

	Yes	No	Explain

6. Are all payments made by serially numbered checks (except where a petty cash fund is used)? _____ _____ _____

7. Is an imprest petty cash fund used? _____ _____ _____

   a. Is it counted on a surprise basis? _____ _____ _____

8. Are bank accounts reconciled monthly? _____ _____ _____

   a. Is a record of the reconciliation maintained? _____ _____ _____

D. INTERNAL CONTROLS RELATED TO RECEIVABLES:

1. Are serially numbered invoices used? _____ _____ _____

2. Are accounts receivable ledger cards reconciled with the control account for receivables on a regular basis? _____ _____ _____

3. Is a sample of cash receipts traced from the accounts receivable ledger cards to the original cash records on a regular basis? _____ _____ _____

4. Are receivables that have been written off approved by the client and segregated from the active accounts? _____ _____ _____

   a. Is documentary evidence of collection efforts filed or attached to ledger cards for review? _____ _____ _____

   b. Are periodic status reports required from the collection agency, and retained? _____ _____ _____

   c. Is a list of adjustments to regular charges maintained? _____ _____ _____

5. Are statements prepared and mailed at least monthly? _____ _____ _____

Exhibit 5-2: Internal Control Checklist—Professional Clients (Continued)

	Yes	No	Explain

E. INTERNAL CONTROLS - GENERAL:

1. Is physical control exercised over the accounting records and documents during nonbusiness hours? _____ _____ _____

2. Are monthly or quarterly comparative income statements prepared in sufficient detail to note significant fluctuations in any revenue or expense account? _____ _____ _____

3. Does an accountant conduct a periodic evaluation? _____ _____ _____

4. Is a written list of accounting instructions and office policies and procedures maintained? _____ _____ _____

   a. Is it current? _____ _____ _____

   b. Is it enforced? _____ _____ _____

   c. Is it germane and understandable? _____ _____ _____

F. INTERNAL CONTROL FOR SECURITIES, INVENTORIES, AND EQUIPMENT:

1. Securities:

   a. Are securities safeguarded? _____ _____ _____

2. Inventories (drugs, supplies, etc.):

   a. Are inventory control records kept? _____ _____ _____

   b. Is limited access allowed to prescription slips? _____ _____ _____

   c. Is inventory periodically reviewed? _____ _____ _____

3. Equipment:

   a. Are equipment purchases adequately justified and financed? _____ _____ _____

Exhibit 5-2: Internal Control Checklist—Professional Clients (Continued)

	Yes	No	Explain

b. Does the client try to determine the incremental revenues or reductions in operating costs compared with the purchase price, the payback period, and means of financing?   _____ _____ _____

c. Is adequate equipment insurance protection maintained?   _____ _____ _____

d. Are small tools safeguarded from theft or is an accurate record kept of such tools?   _____ _____ _____

G. INTERNAL CONTROL FOR TRUST FUNDS

1. Does the client have trust funds?   _____ _____ _____

2. Are trust funds segregated from other funds?   _____ _____ _____

3. Is there a clear record of funds received and funds disbursed?   _____ _____ _____

4. Is there a client ledger clearly reflecting all transactions of each client?   _____ _____ _____

5. Is there a monthly reconciliation of client balances against the funds on hand?   _____ _____ _____

Exhibit 5-2: Internal Control Checklist—Professional Clients (Continued)

Internal Controls Related to Personnel

1. Employees having access to cash should be bonded.
2. Vacations should be mandatory for all employees
3. Careful investigation should be made before hiring.

Internal Controls Related to Cash

4. One person should be assigned responsibility for handling cash.
5. A system of prenumbered receipts should be in use for receipt of incoming funds.
6. Cash receipts should be deposited intact daily.
7. The bank should be instructed in writing not to cash checks payable to the client.
8. Disbursements should be made by prenumbered check.
9. Petty cash should be under an imprest system.
10. Bank accounts should be reconciled monthly.

Internal Controls Related to Receivables

11. For clients making charges based on office visits a system of prenumbered slips should be used to account for such visits.
12. A procedure should be in place whereby the accountant or another designated person samples cash receipts and receivables records on a regular basis.
13. The client should personally approve receivables to be written off, and such accounts should be segregated from active accounts.
14. Billings should be done promptly and systematically each month.

General Elements of Internal Control

15. Office procedures should be in writing.
16. The system should be evaluated periodically by the accountant.
17. Monthly operating statements should be prepared in sufficient detail so that fluctuations from prior periods can be detected.

Exhibit 5-3: Elements of Internal Control

LONG, CHILTON, PAYTE & HARDIN

Basic Inquiries Checklist
Review of Financial Statements

Client Number_____

Name of Client_____

Checklist Prepared by_____Date_____

Checklist Reviewed by_____Date_____

USE OF CHECKLIST:

This checklist should be completed on all engagements when we present unaudited financial statements in compliance with the standards set forth for a "Review of Financial Statements." This does not include those unaudited financial statements presented under the standards of "Compilation."

The checklist is intended to assist in obtaining information without independent audit verification adequate to meet the requirements set out by the AICPA "Statement on Standards for Accounting and Review Services: Compilation and Review of Financial Statements."

Yes or an affirmative answer in all cases is the desired answer. Any no or negative response should be pursued by further inquiry and commented on and cleared with the partner-in-charge if satisfactory resolution cannot be reached. An answer of N/A (not applicable) is satisfactory if appropriate.

This checklist should be present in the current year file along with the Vertical Review and Report Questionnaires.

Information source column should be completed by indicating by number the source as follows:

1. Information incuded in our workpapers arising from analysis of accounts (W/P reference may be included).
2. Information included in memoranda in our workpapers (W/P reference may be included).
3. Information obtained from management and employees. (Identification of source and position should be made.)

Inquiries	Answer	Information Source	Comments
A. General:			
1. Was the trial balance prepared from the general ledger or, if prepared by the client, footed and traced to the general ledger?	_____	_____	_____

Exhibit 5-4: Checklist for Review of Financial Statements

Inquiries	Answer	Information Source	Comments

A. General
   (Continued):

2. Were accrual basis, generally accepted accounting principles applied during the year on a basis consistent with the preceding year?   _____ _____ _____

B. Cash:

1. Have bank balances been reconciled to the general ledger balances?   _____ _____ _____

2. Have old outstanding checks or unusual items in the bank reconciliation been reviewed and adjustments made where necessary?   _____ _____ _____

3. Has a proper cutoff of cash transactions been made and adjustments made where necessary, including back-dated checks and deposits in transit or undeposited receipts?   _____ _____ _____

4. Have petty cash and change funds been counted and reconciled to general ledger control accounts?   _____ _____ _____

5. Are there restrictions relative to any of the cash balances?   _____ _____ _____

C. Receivables:

1. Has a listing of the individual subsidiary accounts been prepared and reconciled to the general ledger control account?   _____ _____ _____

2. Have credit balance accounts been totaled and reclassification as a payable considered or been accomplished?   _____ _____ _____

3. Have receivables from employees, officers, directors, stockholders, subsidiaries, and other affiliates been disclosed separately?   _____ _____ _____

4. Has an adequate allowance been made for doubtful accounts?   _____ _____ _____

Exhbit 5-4: Checklist for Review of Financial Statements (Continued)

	Answer	Information Source	Comments

Inquiries

C. Receivables (Continued):

5. Have receivables that are considered to be uncollectible by management been written off? _____ _____ _____

6. If interest requirements on loans and accounts are present, has interest been properly reflected? _____ _____ _____

7. Has there been an adequate cutoff of sales transactions? _____ _____ _____

8. a) Have any receivables been pledged, discounted or factored? _____ _____ _____

   b) If so, has proper disclosure been made? _____ _____ _____

D. Inventories:

1. Has a physical count of the inventory been made? _____ _____ _____

2. If not physically counted, do we have documentation, and is it a valid, acceptable method? _____ _____ _____

3. Have the general ledger control accounts been adjusted to agree with the physical inventories? _____ _____ _____

4. If physical count was taken at a date other than the statement date, were adequate procedures used to adjust inventory values to the statement date? _____ _____ _____

5. If consignments existed, were they properly reflected in the physical inventories? _____ _____ _____

6. Have write-downs for obsolescence or cost in excess of realizable value been made if appropriate? _____ _____ _____

7. Has an acceptable method of valuation been used on a consistent basis? _____ _____ _____

8. Has there been an adequate cut-off of purchases, goods in transit, and returned goods? _____ _____ _____

Exhibit 5-4: Checklist for Review of Financial Statements (Continued)

Inquiries	Answer	Information Source	Comments

. D. <u>Inventories</u> (Continued):

9. a) Has any of the inventory been pledged or encumbered? _____ _____ _____

b) If so, has proper disclosure been made? _____ _____ _____

E. <u>Prepaid Expenses and Deferred Charges</u>:

1. Are amounts per general ledger in agreement with schedules maintained at statement date? _____ _____ _____

2. Is amortization in accordance with generally accepted methods? _____ _____ _____

3. Do balances appear reasonable and proper at statement date? _____ _____ _____

F. <u>Investments</u>:

1. Are amounts per general ledger in agreement with schedules maintained or prepared at statement date? _____ _____ _____

2. Have amounts recorded as income been scheduled with investment and compared to amounts earned? _____ _____ _____

3. Have gains and losses on sales of investments been properly reflected? _____ _____ _____

4. Has there been a proper classification between current and noncurrent assets? _____ _____ _____

5. Have market values been obtained and listed and compared to carrying basis and recorded where appropriate? _____ _____ _____

6. Where investments in affiliated companies are present, have proper consolidation or equity methods of accounting been reflected? _____ _____ _____

G. <u>Property, Plant and Equipment</u>:

1. Do the general ledger balances in the various property, plant and equipment accounts agree with detailed depreciation schedules or equipment records? _____ _____ _____

Exhibit 5-4: Checklist for Review of Financial Statements (Continued)

Inquiries	Answer	Information Source	Comments

G. Property, Plant and Equipment (Continued):

2. Do the accounting records reflect original cost of the fixed assets and the accumulated depreciation based upon this cost?

3. Are consistent capitalization criteria being applied?

4. Are lives assigned and depreciation methods being applied consistently, appropriately and reasonably?

5. Have all retirements through sales, trades or other disposals been properly reflected in the accounting records?

6. Have all material capital leases been reflected properly on the records?

7. Have any of the fixed assets been mortgaged, pledged, or encumbered in any way?

H. Other Assets:

1. Do the general ledger accounts reflect the cost of intangible assets and deferred charges and consistent, appropriate and reasonable amortization methods?

2. Are schedules of amortization of the cost of appropriate assets being maintained and balanced to the general ledger account?

3. Are other assets being properly classified between current and noncurrent?

I. Notes Payable:

1. Have schedules been prepared showing amounts, interest rates, collateral, terms of payment, etc., and balanced to the general ledger control accounts?

Exhibit 5-4: Checklist for Review of Financial Statements (Continued)

Inquiries	Answer	Information Source	Comments

I. Notes Payable (Continued):

2. Are notes due to officers, stockholders, employees, directors, and affiliates separately stated and reflected?

3. Is interest expense being properly reflected?

4. Are there any restrictive covenants in existence and are they being complied with?

5. Has proper classification been made between current and long-term payables?

J. Accounts Payable:

1. Have payables been listed and balanced to the general ledger control accounts?

2. Have amounts due to officers, stockholders, employees, directors, and affiliates been segregated and listed?

3. Have material debit balance account payables been totaled and reclassified as receivables?

4. Have all material accounts payable been reflected?

K. Accrued Expenses:

1. Have all significant accruals, such as payroll, interest, and contribution to pension and profit-sharing plans been reflected?

2. Are amounts reflected supported by schedules and are computations of the amounts consistent, appropriate, and reasonable?

L. Income Tax Provisions:

1. Has provision been made for current and prior year Federal and State income taxes?

Exhibit 5-4: Checklist for Review of Financial Statements (Continued)

Inquiries	Answer	Information Source	Comments

L.   Income Tax Provisions (Continued):

2. Are all assessments and amounts due to examinations by Federal and State agencies reflected? _____ _____ _____

3. a) Are there any timing differences? _____ _____ _____
   b) Are proper deferred taxes reflected? _____ _____ _____

4. Are appropriate schedules maintained on investment credit and net operating loss carryback and carryovers? _____ _____ _____

M. Other Liabilities:

1. Have proper provisions been made for any contingent liabilities, such as discounted notes, drafts, endorsements, warrants, litigations, and unsettled asserted claims or potential unasserted claims? _____ _____ _____

2. Has pertinent information been disclosed relative to any material contractual obligations for construction or purchase of real property and equipment and any commitments or options to purchase or sell company securities? _____ _____ _____

N. Equity:

1. Have schedules of stockholders and shares outstanding been updated and kept current and balanced to the general ledger control accounts? _____ _____ _____

2. If the company has acquired treasury stock, is it properly accounted for in the accounts and reflected at cost? _____ _____ _____

3. Have all stock repurchase agreements and stock preferences and options been properly reflected and disclosed? _____ _____ _____

O. Income and Expense:

1. Are sales and revenues from sale of products or services recognized in the appropriate accounting period? _____ _____ _____

Exhibit 5-4: Checklist for Review of Financial Statements (Continued)

	Information	
Inquiries	Answer Source	Comments

O.   Income and Expense
        (Continued):

1. Are sales and revenues from sale of products or services recognized in the appropriate accounting period?   _____   _____   _____

2. Are purchases and expenses recognized in the appropriate period and properly classified on a consistent basis with prior periods?   _____   _____   _____

3. Are extraordinary items properly stated separately in the accounting records?   _____   _____   _____

Exhibit 5-4: Checklist for Review of Financial Statements (Continued)

To The Partners of
Putnam & Johnson
Brownsville, Texas

We have examined the financial statements of Putnam & Johnson for the year ended June 30, 19X1, and have issued our report thereon dated August 20, 19X1. As a part of our examination we made a study and evaluation of the system of internal accounting control as required by generally accepted auditing standards. Under these standards, the purpose of such an evaluation is to establish a basis for reliance on the system of internal accounting control in determining the nature, timing, and extent of other auditing procedures that are necessary for expressing an opinion on the financial statements and to assist the auditor in planning and performing his examination of the financial statements.

Our examination of the financial statements was made in accordance with generally accepted auditing standards, including the study and evaluation of the system of internal accounting control, made for the purposes set forth in the preceding paragraph. Such study would not necessarily disclose all weaknesses in the system because it was based on selective tests of accounting records and related data. However, we submit the following comments and recommendations which we believe would improve the internal accounting and administrative control of the partnership.

CASH

Cash Receipts

Cash received in payment of receivables is ultimately given to the accounting department for deposit in the bank. This causes a weakness in internal control because people responsible for entering the receipt onto the books also have access to the cash.

Recommendation

A person outside of the accounting department should be designated to receive all incoming payments. This person then should make a listing of the daily receipts, with an appropriate time cutoff. The listing and the checks or cash should be given to a partner for comparison of actual receipts to the listing. After this comparison the cash and checks should be given to the person responsible for making the deposit. The listing should be given to the accounting department for posting to the books. When the validated deposit slips are received the accounting department should compare the listings to the actual deposit.

PERSONNEL

Vacations

Some employees take only a few days' vacation at a time. Failure to require employees to take their full vacation at one time could lead to the concealing of irregularities on the part of some employees.

Recommendation

All employees should be required to take their full vacation at one time or in segments of two separate weeks.

Exhibit 5-5: Management Letter to a Professional Client

Related Employees

Related employees should not work within the same department. Related employees are more likely to aid each other in the concealing of any irregularities that might arise.

Recommendation

Further hiring of related employees should be discontinued. Any current related employees should be separated into different department or function areas.

SEGREGATION OF DUTIES

Personnel Records

Personnel records are being maintained by the same employees who are responsible for preparing and distributing payroll checks. This could lead to the introduction of fictitious employees into the payroll cycle.

Recommendation

The payroll checks should be separated from the personnel records. The duties of maintaining personnel files and preparation and distribution of payroll checks should be separated.

Bank Reconciliation

The payroll bank account is reconciled by the person responsible for preparing and distributing payroll checks. This could lead to the concealing of irregularities on the part of the employees involved.

Recommendation

The duties of reconciling the payroll bank account and the preparation of payroll checks should be separated.

DISBURSEMENTS

Cancellation of invoices

Some invoices were not cancelled completely. Duplicate payment of these invoices could result.

Recommendation

All pages of invoices and any supporting documents should be stamped PAID with the date of payment indicated on said invoice or other document.

OTHER RECOMMENDATIONS

Reconciliation of Accounts Receivable

Accounts receivable should be reconciled on a regular basis. Consideration should be given to computerizing receivables records to provide better control and reporting.

Exhibit 5-5: Management Letter to a Professional Client (Continued)

Review of Accounts Receivable

A review of accounts receivable should be made on a regular basis to facilitate collection follow-up.

At year end when uncollectible accounts are charged off, the expenses advanced to clients should be segregated and handled as a tax-deductible expense.

TRUSTEE LIABILITY ACCOUNTS

Personal Usage

A partner has used trust funds for personal use. The money was paid back at a later date.

Recommendation

No one should be allowed to use trust funds for any but the designated use.

Debit Balances

There are several debit balances reflected in the trustee liability accounts. Other debit balances have accrued during the year.

Recommendation

There should never be debit balances in the trustee liability accounts, since it signifies that one client's funds have been improperly used in behalf of another client.

CONCLUSION

The objective of internal accounting control is to provide reasonable, but not absolute, assurance on the safeguarding of assets against loss from unauthorized use or disposition and the reliability of financial records for preparing financial statements and maintaining accountability for assets. The concept of reasonable assurance recognizes that the cost of a system of internal accounting control should not exceed the benefits derived and also recognizes that the evaluation of these factors necessarily requires estimates and judgments by management.

There are inherent limitations that should be recognized in considering the potential effectiveness of any system of internal accounting control. In the performance of most control procedures, errors can result from misunderstanding of instructions, mistakes of judgment, carelessness or other personal factors. Control procedures whose effectiveness depends upon segregation of duties can be circumvented by collusion. Further, projection of any evaluation of internal accounting control to future periods is subject to the risk that the procedures may become inadequate because of changes in conditions, and the degree of compliance with the procedures may deteriorate.

Respectfully submitted,

LONG, CHILTON, PAYTE & HARDIN
Certified Public Accountants

Exhibit 5-5: Management Letter to a Professional Client (Continued)

6

Effective Income Tax Service

The professional client usually employs an accountant initially because he or she needs help with income tax matters. Income tax service provides the catalyst for other services. It must be thorough, professional and first class in every respect. The client who feels he or she is receiving first class income tax service usually requests assistance in other areas.

EDUCATING THE CLIENT ABOUT TAXES

The best income tax service is provided those clients who have been educated regarding tax matters. They have learned to anticipate tax problems, are aware of the need for staying in touch with their accountant and realize the importance of consulting about the tax effect of transactions in advance. This education process requires both patience and initiative on the part of the accountant, and is a responsibility he or she should assume. Unfortunately, lessons about tax planning are frequently learned from costly experiences.

The education process starts by discussing with the client items of income and deductions affecting tax liability. Explain procedures the client should follow for developing the necessary information for his or her tax return. Be sure that the client is fully aware of all possible deductions, both business and nonbusiness.

The client must learn the importance of adequate records and the need for verification of various items. If the professional practice receives a considerable amount of income by way of cash receipts, the client must understand the importance of having a system for accounting for cash receipts that will satisfy the IRS.

Explain the importance of keeping business transactions separate from personal transactions. Some professional people tend to write checks from whatever account is most convenient or has available funds. Others let their spouses pay certain deductible expenses out of personal bank accounts. Make every effort to head off these problems in advance.

Making Your Client Tax Conscious

Stress with clients at every opportunity the need to advise you of major transactions. Every experienced practitioner can relate stories of clients who entered into major transactions without planning. Give the client a hypothetical example of such a case and the serious tax consequences. Many clients are strongly motivated and like to take action quickly, but an expensive mistake generally makes them tax conscious.

The accountant should take initiative in seeing that tax planning is done on a timely basis. The tax conscious client will probably want to review the situation two or three times during the year. If he or she is planning to make tax shelter investments, the planning and review process should start at a sufficiently early date so that investments don't have to be made at the last minute. Tax planning sessions later in the year are important, also, to assist the client in planning for charitable contributions, retirement fund deductions, selling assets to establish gains and losses, etc.

The accountant should strive to set up a schedule of tax planning sessions during the year. One practical approach to this is to schedule a session immediately prior to each estimated tax payment date. The client who is incorporated and on a salary with withholding tax will be likely to need a different schedule. The most important tax planning for this client usually takes place just prior to the corporate year end (see Chapter 7).

These reviews will provide an opportunity to plan ahead for putting money into retirement, making tax shelter investments, and incorporating the practice. This service is most important; it cannot be stressed too strongly.

TAX DEDUCTIONS REQUIRING SPECIAL CARE

A majority of the professional client's deductions such as salaries, rent and utilities are of a nature that are easily verified and not likely to be questioned. There are other deductions, however, that must be handled very carefully, or the deduction could be lost because of inadequate records or verification. Some of these are discussed below.

Professional Meetings, Seminars and Conventions

Nearly all professional clients attend professional meetings. This practice is becoming more widespread because of the increasing need for continuing professional education. Many meetings and seminars are held in resort areas or foreign locations, raising the question as to whether the trip is actually a bona fide business meeting or a disguised vacation.

Foreign travel has certain requirements built into the tax law, making it more difficult to qualify for a tax deduction than is the case with domestic travel. The accountant must be alert to any foreign travel plans of his professional clients and make them aware of the restrictions that apply.

In connection with meetings held at well-known resorts or aboard a cruise ship, there is a possibility that the deduction could be questioned as a disguised vacation. The IRS will very likely scrutinize such meetings to determine the actual facts. The expenses will not be disallowed because of the site of the meeting, but because the business activities were insignificant in relation to the recreational activities.

Professional clients attending meetings in resort areas should be advised to bring back the program activities, which should reflect a significant amount of time spent in business sessions.

Advise the client of the need to document travel expenses by retaining airline tickets, hotel bills, etc. Remind him that the use of credit cards or checks is preferable to payment in cash. Charging meals on credit cards or to the hotel account makes it much easier to verify these expenditures. Advise him to limit his cash expenditures to such items as tips, taxis, parking, and the like.

Continuing education expenditures are deductible for any practitioner who is maintaining or improving the skills required in his profession. The client should be advised about the kinds of expenses that do and do not qualify, and how to substantiate his deductions.

Business Promotion and Entertainment

Every accountant is familiar with the problems and pitfalls related to deducting expenses in this area. Professional clients must be made aware of requirements that entertainment be properly substantiated and directly related to a business activity.

High-income professional clients have been known to come up with another idea for business promotion and entertainment: that of charging off expenses relating to airplanes, pleasure boats, resort condominiums, and the like. Persuading the client to agree to a reasonable solution to this problem can be a real challenge. Needless to say, IRS rules regarding "entertainment facilities" must be brought to the client's attention clearly and emphatically.

Some professional clients don't like to bother with the details of documenting entertainment records with the names of guests and the nature of the business discussion. A client with the inclination to charge off large entertainment expenses must, again, be made aware of these requirements clearly and emphatically.

OFFICE IN THE HOME

Professional clients frequently maintain an office at home. For some, it is their main office—for many, however, it is a second office, used for weekend or evening work, or a place to work when they need to get away from their regular office and work without interruption.

IRS requirements for deduction of expenses relating to an office in the home are stringent. Such deductions are not permitted except to the extent that they are attributable to the portion of the home used exclusively and on a regular basis as:

- The principal place of business, or
- A place of business which is used by patients or clients in meeting or dealing with the taxpayer in the normal course of business.

Exclusive use of the portion of the home means a specific area must be used solely for the purpose of carrying on the business. Using the area for both business and personal use will not satisfy the requirements. For example, a den used as a place to write legal briefs will not qualify if the taxpayer or his family also use the den for personal purposes.

The accountant dealing with professional clients must be sufficiently familiar with these requirements to advise his clients and particularly keep them from attempting to claim deductions that are clearly not permitted.

HELPING THE CLIENT DIVERT TAXABLE INCOME TO OTHERS

A high-income professional client can save significant income taxes by diverting taxable income to others, preferably to family members who are in a lower tax bracket.

Use of a Trust

The most commonly used technique for diverting income is putting revenue-producing assets into trust, with family members named as beneficiaries of the trust and receiving the income. This is a particularly effective tool for the client with children approaching college age. Investment income can be diverted to the children, who can use it for their college costs. The best time to set up the trust is before the college years begin, so that funds can be accumulated before and during these years.

The kinds of expenses to be paid from trust income must be watched carefully. The parent will be taxable for payment of children's expenses which the parent is legally obligated as a parent to pay. Sending a child to college is not generally considered a legal parental obligation and college costs normally occur after the child has reached legal age, thus they can be paid from trust income. In addition to college expenses, such "extras" as summer camp and foreign travel have been paid from trust income and considered beyond the legal obligation of the parent. The payment of food, clothing, shelter and precollege education expenses should be avoided, however.

The type of assets to put into the trust must be carefully considered. The professional client should not attempt to divert income from his own professional efforts to the trust, either directly or in some disguised form. The trust must be funded with investment assets that produce current income. The best choices of investment assets are stocks, bonds, real estate, investments in limited partnerships, etc., that are unrelated to the professional practice. Investments producing tax charge-offs should be retained by the client, of course.

Some professionals own their office buildings and put them in trust. Others utilize professional office equipment for this purpose. This is an attractive arrangement that produces excellent tax results.

Some words of caution are needed, however. The IRS may challenge such an arrangement because the professional is still enjoying effective use and control of the asset. Federal courts in different parts of the country have reached different opinions on this matter. Some courts have held that there is no business purpose to such an arrangement; others have found the trust arrangement valid.

The accountant should do these things when considering such a trust arrangement for a client:

- Become familiar with the position of the courts in his area on the matter.
- Evaluate the risk of IRS challenge of the trust arrangement.
- Fully brief the client on the potential for problems with IRS. It is wise to put this in writing. If the client decides to go ahead in face of possible IRS challenge it is important for the accountant to have a written record of words of caution provided.

What term of trust should be set up? Many professionals don't want to divest themselves of income-producing assets forever; they want to enjoy the income themselves in later years. In this case a trust with a limited term of years should be used. To meet IRS requirements, the trust must run for ten years and one day, minimum. Commonly known as Clifford trusts, these are a popular device for diverting income. At the end of the trust period the assets are returned to the original owner.

A Clifford trust does not effectively remove the assets from the client's estate, however. If the trust is to serve as an estate planning tool, an irrevocable trust is required. The client is faced with the decision of whether to take the assets back later for income purposes, or to give them up permanently for estate tax purposes.

The choice of a trustee is an important factor. Some clients want to serve as their own trustees, while others choose an outside trustee. If the client serves as trustee there is risk that the IRS will allege that effective control of the property was not given up. When the client serves as trustee, his powers should be as limited as possible. The broader the trustee's powers (to sprinkle income among several beneficiaries, for example) the more likely is an IRS challenge.

When considering the appointment of a trustee the client needs to be aware of the cost factors. Financial institutions have a minimum fee, which can be a major expense for a small trust. Some professionals setting up a trust that requires limited effort on the part of the trustee appoint a friend, relative, attorney, or accountant to serve. Using such an individual could be questioned by the IRS, since the trustee must be independent and not subject to the control of the grantor. Such arrangements are, nevertheless, preferable to having the grantor himself serve as trustee.

The client must be made to understand that the trust is a separate legal and taxable entity and must be operated with that in mind. The trust's funds must not be commingled with those of the grantor or anyone else, proper accounting records must be maintained, and necessary tax returns filed. Under no circumstances should the trust's funds be used for the benefit of the grantor, or loaned to him or her. Such an action will inevitably lead to an IRS holding that the client is enjoying the income and should be taxed on it.

One final note: the gift of property to a trust normally gives rise to a taxable gift and the filing of a gift tax return. This is true of a ten-year trust as well as an irrevocable trust. Be sure the client is aware of this requirement before making a decision to go ahead.

To summarize, a trust can effectively divert income to others and save significant income taxes. It should be used at the right time and with the right assets. It must be set up and administered as a separate entity. The accountant should help the client determine if this is the way to go and work with the client in setting up and administering the trust.

The tax benefits of a trust should be provided to the client in writing in a clear, concise format. See Exhibit 6-1 for an example.

USE OF A CORPORATION

A tax planning device used to some extent is a corporation set up to own certain assets used in the professional practice; i.e., the building or the equipment. The corporation leases these assets to the practice, diverting taxable income into low bracket corporate rates.

The corporate stock may be owned by the practitioner or by members of his or her family. The family members would normally be children, but in some cases would be parents or others for whom the client has financial responsibility.

The corporation has as its principal advantage the accumulation of taxable income at low tax rates. A distinct disadvantage is the problem of getting money out of the corporation. If the practitioner is the stockholder he or she could probably justify some salary or directors fees, but at a 50% tax bracket in his or her personal return. Children or parents would have difficulty justifying any compensation.

It is possible to retain earnings in the corporation for a period of years and then dissolve the corporation when the client sells out or retires. Computations should be made to ascertain the tax advantages, if any, after considering both the annual corporation income tax and the personal tax on dissolution.

In considering a corporation, attention should be given to whether a valid business purpose exists. If the IRS determines that the corporation was set up strictly for tax saving purposes and has no valid business purpose, the income might be taxed back to the professional client.

Corporations are less flexible than trusts and have not received widespread use in tax planning for professional clients. There may be instances, however, where a corporation would be appropriate and, therefore, this tool should be considered in the right circumstances.

RETIREMENT PLANS FOR SELF-EMPLOYED PROFESSIONALS

An important area of tax planning for professional clients involves getting them into the right retirement plan at the right time. This discussion deals only with self-employment retirement plans (corporate retirement plans will be discussed in Chapter 7 in connection with professional corporations).

The Keogh Plan for self-employed persons is suitable for many professional clients. Contributions can be made up to $30,000 per year, which will be as much as some clients will want to contribute. The Keogh Plan requires that all employees with over three years' employment be covered with immediate coverage and vesting. There is no flexibility in regard to employee coverage or vesting, as there is in corporate plans.

The professional client in his or her early days of practice must be cautioned to avoid getting into a Keogh Plan too early. First, financial commitments may be such that he or she does not have the extra cash to put into retirement. Second, if the client goes into a Keogh Plan before being in practice three years, the actual time in practice will determine the waiting period for covering employees.

> Example: Dr. Jones has been in practice eighteen months and decides to go into a Keogh Plan. The waiting period for entering her plan, therefore, is established at eighteen months for her employees. If she wants to establish a three-year waiting period for her employees she should establish the plan after she has been in practice three years.

Many organizations sell IRA plans and/or Keogh Plans as part of a package. The accountant should offer to review such proposals for the client. The various programs offer a wide range of return and risk, as well as varying sales charges. All such points should be reviewed carefully so that an intelligent decision can be made as to the type of program that suits the client's situation best.

The tax benefits from making retirement contributions should be given the client in writing and in a concise, easy-to-understand format. See Exhibit 7-1 for an example.

HELPING THE CLIENT WITH TAX SHELTER INVESTMENTS

Tax shelter investments have become popular in recent years and high-income professionals are promising targets for those selling such investments. What could be more inviting than to invest some excess funds in something that will provide a good return and save taxes at the same time?

Unfortunately, such investments don't always produce magic results and the accountant needs to be in a position to offer some basic guidance on what to expect. Many accountants don't feel qualified to give investment advice and should not do so. In fact, the accountant should avoid making specific recommendations as to whether the client should go into a particular investment. Instead he should evaluate the soundness, risk, and potential tax effect of the investment.

For many professional clients the accountant is the only impartial advisor available to assist with such investment decisions. These clients want to take advantage of tax shelters and to make sound investments. They are attracted to proposals for tax shelter investments, but are suspicious of the salesman who earns a commission from selling it. The professional client, therefore, generally welcomes the opportunity to discuss such proposals with the accountant.

Points on Which to Caution the Client

The first point to emphasize is that investments are for the purpose of making money, not saving taxes. A profitable investment will require the payment of taxes at some point. The payment of taxes may be postponed for several years, and may result in long-term capital gain income, but if the investment is profitable, the tax benefits are a deferral, not a permanent saving. To put it another way, the client shouldn't get so enthused about tax saving that he disregards the quality of the investment.

Another potential pitfall related to tax shelter investments is the service offered to professional clients by some organizations involving promotion of tax shelter investments to get the client's attention. Professional clients are generally very busy and sometimes naive in business and investment matters. If someone offers to save them taxes they are impressed and receptive to additional services (such as retirement plan and financial advisory services). Some professional clients become almost totally reliant on advisers whose income is derived from commissions on sales of investments.

While these arrangements are not always detrimental to the client, there is no doubt some professionals follow the recommendations of such advisers to the extent that they give up control and responsibility for their own financial affairs. An accountant who has a close working relationship with professional clients can, in conjunction with other advisers, serve the clients so that they make their own decisions and control their own destinies. This generally gives better results and is in the clients' best interest.

Evaluating the Investment

The accountant should have some general guidelines regarding questionable investments and danger signals to be on guard against. Here are several danger signals:

1. Properties located a great distance away or in a remote location
2. An investment offered at the last minute during the tax year and emphasizing great tax savings
3. An investment whose only purpose is saving taxes and which does not have a sound business purpose standing alone
4. An investment in which the operator commingles many operations out of one office in a manner that makes it difficult to evaluate how each is doing
5. An investment with a complicated structure that may have been set up to make it difficult for the IRS to examine.

There are a number of steps the accountant can take to become familiar with the investment. These include carefully reviewing the prospectus, making independent inquiries to obtain significant facts about the property and its promoters, and physically examining the project. One of the best evaluation steps is to find out if the promoters are reliable.

It is helpful to the accountant to develop a relationship with someone knowledgeable in the investment field with whom he can consult. A working relationship with someone in a brokerage concern, for example, can provide the accountant with valuable insight into investment proposals and the reputation of its promoters.

The accountant should have certain tax shelter investments about which he is knowledgeable and that he can recommend to clients. A contact in a brokerage firm can provide prospectuses for the accountant to give to clients when the occasion arises. The accountant who can provide suggestions for sound investments to clients is providing an important and appreciated service.

Pitfalls of Drastic Fluctuations in Income

Tax shelter investments often give rise to drastic fluctuations in income. Most tax shelter investments are sold on the premise of large tax deductions in the early years. If the investment proves successful, however, taxable income will result in due time.

One problem the client should be made aware of is the potential for a large tax liability in the year the investment is sold. The accountant should prepare the client for this situation by projecting the potential tax liability on the sale. It is possible the entire sales proceeds, or more, could be offset by the tax liability.

Projecting the tax effect of an investment that will run over a period of years is difficult to do, but the accountant can use his judgment and experience to come up with figures that will give the client an idea of what lies ahead.

An example of this type of analysis of a tax shelter investment is found in Exhibit 6-2.

TAX CONSIDERATIONS WHEN BUYING OR SELLING A PROFESSIONAL PRACTICE

From time to time the accountant is called upon to advise the professional on the purchase or sale of a practice. This may develop in several ways: an established practitioner wants to expand through the purchase of a practice; a young professional wants to establish himself or herself by buying a practice; a long-time client decides to sell out and retire.

Tax planning is essential in working out the terms of the purchase or sale, and the accountant should arrange to be closely involved in the negotiations. The approach taken by the accountant will vary and will depend on such factors as the business knowledge of the parties involved, and the role of attorneys and their tax expertise. The accountant's role will primarily be influenced, however, by whether he or she represents the buyer or the seller. The buyer and seller have adverse interests, to some extent at least, in the tax effect of the transaction and the the accountant must be fully conscious of these differences.

A matter of primary concern in tax planning is the allocation of the purchase price. This allocation can provide significant tax advantages to the buyer, and vice versa, and can increase or decrease the seller's tax liability. What works to the advantage of one party, unfortunately, frequently has the opposite effect on the other.

To use an example, let's assume that Dr. Smith, a long standing veterinarian client, advises you he is negotiating to sell his practice and asks for tax advice. The buyer and his accountant have proposed an allocation of the $200,000 price as follows:

Equipment	$35,000 (initial cost $50,000 - book value $20,000)
Goodwill	30,000
Agreement not to compete	75,000 (five-year period)
Customer list	60,000
	$200,000

Dr. Smith does not understand the tax effect of these items, and wants you to study them and review them with him.

It is apparent that the allocation has been weighted heavily toward the agreement not to compete and the customer list. A strong argument can be made that the equipment and goodwill are of more value than has been assigned, and the other two items have less value. You explain the following tax results to Dr. Smith:

> The gain of $15,000 on sale of equipment is all ordinary income due to depreciation recapture and any higher allocation of selling price (up to $50,000) would increase ordinary income. Long-term capital gain would arise only if the equipment is sold for more than $50,000.

> Goodwill is long-term capital gain, regardless of the price. It is not depreciable to the buyer, who wants to purchase it at the lowest possible price.

> The agreement not to compete is ordinary income to Dr. Smith, who should insist that it be valued as conservatively as possible. The buyer can write it off over its five-year life.

> The customer list is depreciable by the buyer, but provides long-term gain to Dr. Smith. On this item the parties do not have an adverse interest and can agree to allocate as much as possible. The valuation of a customer list, however, is very subjective and subject to IRS challenge.

There are two points that should be pursued in Dr. Smith's behalf:

> If the fair market value of the equipment exceeds $50,000, efforts should be made to get the allocation adjusted so Dr. Smith can enjoy the long-term capital gain to which he is entitled.

> The agreement not to compete should be valued as conservatively as possible. There are few guidelines as to how to measure the value of such an agreement, but every effort should be made to minimize the ordinary income attributed to this item.

The other two items (goodwill and customer list) are capital gain items to Dr. Smith, so any change in the allocation would have no tax effect. Every effort should be made, regardless, to value each item realistically.

The buyer generally has more at stake in the allocation than the seller. The buyer is trying to accomplish two things;

1. Avoid or minimize the allocation to goodwill, which is not depreciable.

2. Allocate the purchase to those items that will provide the shortest period for write-off.

The accountant representing the buyer must obtain the best tax treatment possible, but must guard against making unreasonable and arbitrary allocations. In the above case, for example, the allocation of $60,000 to customer lists may very well be challenged and set up by the IRS as goodwill. It is tempting to keep goodwill at a minimum and the urge to do this can lead to unreasonable allocations.

HANDLING OF INCOME TAX EXAMINATIONS

An important service for an accountant is assisting the client with an income tax examination. In this situation, most clients feel on the defensive and are uncomfortable dealing with an Internal Revenue Agent. Many clients prefer that their accountant handle as much of the work in connection with the examination as possible.

One important ingredient in dealing successfully with Internal Revenue agents is to have their respect before the examination begins. Your own reputation as a tax practitioner establishes the degree of respect you can command. If you are known as an accountant who strives to get all the information from the client and who prepares returns responsibly, your effectiveness will be greatly increased. Agents are also impressed by the accountant who has an adequate tax library and a good command of tax law.

You cannot expect, of course, to settle all problems with Internal Revenue agents based only on your reputation. There will always be honest differences of opinion in interpreting factual situations, tax laws and regulations. The agent who respects your ability, however, is likely to raise only those issues that have merit and is not likely to harass the client or try to take advantage of him or her.

It is important during an examination to provide the Internal Revenue agent with good records that can be easily reviewed. A good set of records and files in which paid bills and other material can be easily located speeds up the agent's work. An agent who finds records and supporting data in good order will often complete the examination in a short period of time with less likelihood of raising questions.

On the other hand, an agent confronted by poor records and lack of sufficient supporting data can easily become frustrated. This frustration may evidence itself in proposals for additional tax. It is only logical that an agent who has to spend a great deal of time digging through poor records is more likely to present the client with a proposal for additional tax. We, therefore, advise our clients to make every effort to provide the agent with the material he or she wants in the best possible order so that it can be readily reviewed and the examination completed in the shortest possible time.

If you have audited the client, your audit file can be a useful tool during the examination. A good audit file contains information that is helpful to the agent, who can quickly review the trial balance, adjusting entries and the verifications and analyses you have performed on the various accounts. A review of the audit file enables the agent to complete his or her work promptly. This is, in fact, one reason for a client to have an audit.

In connection with providing information to the Internal Revenue agent, always keep in mind that you have no requirement or responsibility to provide any information except that requested. The agent should be given the accounting records and supporting data wanted and should be given forthright answers to the questions asked. The accountant need not provide any more information than is requested and should not make comments that might lead the agent into new areas. There is nothing unethical about this procedure. There are many areas in the tax law in which differences of opinion can arise and where the accountant will recommend a course of action that is favorable to the client. An Internal Revenue agent might decide the same point in favor of the government, thus creating a point of dispute. Keep in mind, therefore, that your job is to give the agent the information requested, but nothing more.

When the agent requests information from your files, it is best to give him or her only the specific items wanted, not the entire file. Your file may contain memos or notes concerning research you have done on certain transactions that would alert the agent to a sensitive point. Generally the agent will request only your file copies of returns or certain work papers, and this is all you should give him or her—not the entire file.

Some firms have their files organized so that copies of returns are in a "tax file" and other material is in a "correspondence file." This arrangement has the advantage of permitting the accountant to give the agent the entire tax file, which contains nothing but copies of returns.

Your dealing with the Internal Revenue agent should always be on professional terms. Even though you have an adversary relationship, it can still be one of friendliness and mutual respect. You should avoid any personal recriminations or heated disputes, which generally work to your disadvantage and your client's. Differences of opinion can be discussed on a professional level, concentrating on the issues at hand rather than on personalities.

Role of the Accountant

Professional clients usually are not interested in the subject of taxes, accounting records, problems with the IRS, and related matters. The one thing that they are least interested in, however, is an IRS examination. This is an unsettling experience which not only makes them uncomfortable but disrupts their schedules and takes up valuable time.

Professional clients are often poorly equipped to deal with an IRS exam; they may talk too much, saying things that could lead the agent into an area that might otherwise be ignored. There is also a risk of a client's becoming antagonistic toward the agent.

The client may not have a suitable place for the agent to work, and probably has neither sufficient time nor expertise to deal effectively with the agent. The situation is one that could very well hinder, rather than help, bring the examination to a satisfactory conclusion.

The accountant, on the other hand, deals with IRS agents regularly on a professional basis. The accountant knows what the agent needs and can deal with him or her objectively and efficiently. From the agent's standpoint dealing with the accountant has the obvious advantage of saving time and minimizing the problems involved. Most agents would prefer to deal with the accountant.

The accountant, therefore, should offer to take primary responsibility for dealing with the agent. If the client authorizes this it will be necessary to obtain a power of attorney from him or her. The agent should be requested to work in the accountant's office rather than the client's. The records will be brought to the accountant's office and questions and inquiries will go through him or her. The client will not be directly involved unless absolutely necessary.

While this method will not work in every case, it has much to be said for it and can be used to good advantage in many instances. It works well for the solo professional practitioner or small group practice where the records can be easily moved to the accountant's office. It probably is not feasible, however, for the examination of a larger professional organization. There will also be instances where either the client or the agent will prefer to conduct the work on the client's premises. Each case will have to be decided on its merits and based on the circumstances.

Procedures to Follow in Handling the Examination

I have followed the practice of handling many examinations that are conducted in our office, as described above. The normal steps followed are along these lines:

1. Have basic material needed by the agent available. This material includes:
   - Client's accounting records
   - Bank statements, deposit slips, and cancelled checks
   - Copies of payroll tax returns and any other items routinely requested by agents
2. Ask the agent to provide a list of other information needed.
3. Comply promptly with agent's requests for supporting invoices and other material.
4. Keep yourself reasonably available to the agent to discuss problems and answer questions. Carry on your normal schedule, but check with the agent periodically.
5. Do everything you can to expedite the examination and move it to a conclusion.

What to Do When You Can't Agree with the Agent

Every effort should be made to reach agreement with the Internal Revenue agent. This is not always possible, however, and the accountant must make a recommendation to the client about appealing the case to a high level. The Internal Revenue Service has appeals officers whose function is to confer with taxpayers and their representatives regarding issues in dispute.

The primary factor to be considered when deciding whether to appeal is the cost involved in relation to the potential benefits. The amount of tax due is a key factor. The client and the accountant must consider the amount of time that will be required to prepare for and attend the conference as well as the distance and travel expense involved. If these amounts seem reasonable in relation to the potential tax benefits, this would indicate a go-ahead. Another factor to be considered is the nature of the issues involved. Some issues can be negotiated and a compromise settlement reached. Other issues are clear black and white; the taxpayer either wins or loses, with no middle ground for negotiation and compromise. If, for example, there is only one issue that cannot be negotiated, it is necessary to evaluate the chances of winning. If the chances of winning are less than fifty-fifty, there is a serious question as to whether to go ahead with the appeal.

Careful preparation must be made for the conference. The accountant should research the cases and rulings on all points in dispute. He must be well prepared regarding both the facts and the tax laws. The appeals officer's job is to settle the case if possible and to give full consideration to a well-prepared presentation. At the same time, the case will not be settled in your favor unless your argument and position are stronger than the agent's.

If there are several issues involved or issues that can be negotiated and compromised, determine in advance the type of compromise you would be willing to accept. Be prepared to suggest a possible compromise settlement at the proper time. In this type of situation, it is almost always possible to reach a settlement that leaves the taxpayer in a better position than the one he or she was in before.

In presenting your case to the appeals officer do not be critical of the agent. You may feel the agent's position is unjustified or disapprove of the manner in which the examination was conducted. These matters are not the responsibility of the appeals officer, however, and there is little he or she can do about it. If anything, you are likely to prejudice your case by criticizing an Internal Revenue Service employee to a colleague. This is not a professional way to handle a tax dispute and should be avoided.

THE HUMAN FACTOR IN TAX WORK

In handling tax work for professional clients remember that each client is an individual whose traits and philosophy must be taken into consideration. You will be dealing with some clients who are very conservative as well as some who are at the opposite end of the spectrum. Some clients are willing to pay their income tax with little complaint, while some are deeply resentful.

Some clients want their tax returns handled conservatively in order to reduce the possibility of IRS examination and to keep their own worries about taxes to a minimum. Others want to do everything possible to reduce taxes and are willing to take certain risks in order to do so.

The tax service and advice given these individuals of widely differing philosophies should vary accordingly—but within limits. The conservative client who wants to minimize his risk and problems should have his tax planning and tax return preparation handled accordingly. The aggressive client should be advised of tax shelters and deductions that can be claimed legitimately—but that the IRS might question.

You should advise the aggressive client of all possible potential deductions, shelters and benefits available. You should also advise this client of the risks of examination along with attendant frustration and time commitment, possible penalties and interest and other negative factors that go along with controversy with the IRS.

Finally—and most important—the aggressive client should be kept in line. There is sometimes a fine line between those actions that can be argued to be within proper interpretation of the tax law and those that slip over the line and become negligence. This line is indistinct at times and each accountant must decide where it falls—then stay sufficiently inside the line to avoid any risk that either he or his client will be charged with negligence.

Aggressive clients sometimes want to stray over the line. The accountant at times must decline to go along. There comes a time when you must tell the client that the idea not only won't work, but it constitutes negligence or even fraud. Make the client aware that your signature is on the return as well as his or hers.

Taking a hard-nosed stance against improper proposals may lose an occasional client, but if so it is a client you are better off without. In most cases the client will realize your position is in his or her best interest and will accord you more respect than before.

In dealing with clients, therefore, treat them as individuals. Tailor your tax service to their individual traits and wishes—but keep them in line with tax law and reality so they won't get into serious trouble.

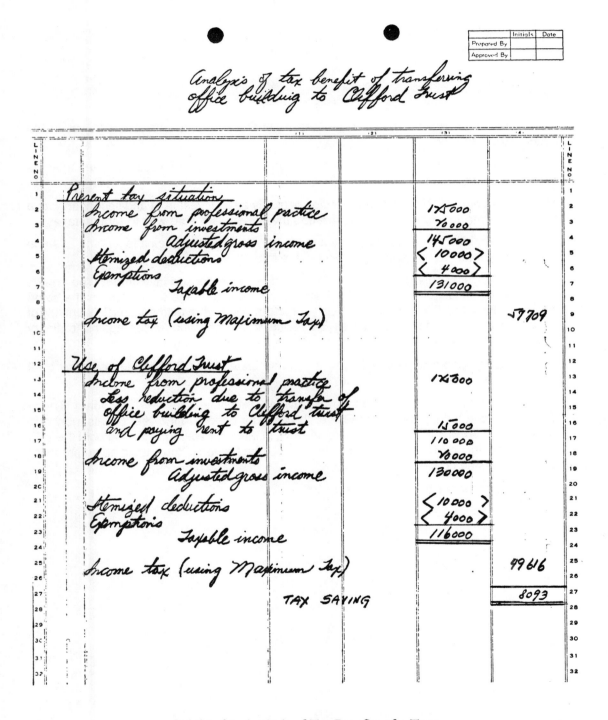

	Initials	Date
Prepared By		
Approved By		

Analysis of tax benefit of transferring office building to Clifford Trust

LINE NO					LINE NO
1	Present tax situation				1
2	Income from professional practice		155000		2
3	Income from investments		70000		3
4	Adjusted gross income		145000		4
5	Itemized deductions		‹10000›		5
6	Exemptions		‹4000›		6
7	Taxable income		131000		7
8					8
9	Income tax (using Maximum Tax)			57709	9
10					10
11					11
12	Use of Clifford Trust				12
13	Income from professional practice		155000		13
14	Less reduction due to transfer of				14
15	office building to Clifford trust				15
16	and paying rent to trust		15000		16
17			110000		17
18	Income from investments		70000		18
19	Adjusted gross income		130000		19
20					20
21	Itemized deductions		‹10000›		21
22	Exemptions		‹4000›		22
23	Taxable income		116000		23
24					24
25	Income tax (using Maximum Tax)			49616	25
26					26
27	TAX SAVING			8093	27
28					28

Exhibit 6-1: Analysis of Tax Benefits of a Trust

Dr. Wilson Weir
Brownsville, Texas

Dear Wilson:

This is written to summarize our discussions regarding a possible investment by you in Tax Shelter Partnership No. 1.

I want to repeat for emphasis certain points regarding tax shelter investments and their tax effect:

- Any investment should be looked upon primarily as an investment and secondarily as a tax shelter (losing money through a bad investment is a sure way to reduce taxes).

- A tax shelter providing a good investment inevitably leads to taxable income at some point, sometimes pyramiding considerable income into one year.

Attached is a schedule reflecting the tax results of this proposed investment. The figures assume, very conservatively, that the investment will be sold in the tenth year for the same amount you invested. Based on these facts your return from the investment consists entirely of your tax saving of $51,186. This tax saving results from deducting losses against ordinary income but reporting most of the gain on the sale as a long-term capital gain.

If the property appreciates in value, which is anticipated, any gain on the investment will more than offset the additional tax due.

The investment provides substantial tax savings, particularly in the early years. These savings are projected to total $100,129 over the ten year period. In the year of sale, however, you will have a tax of $48,943 on the gain. Further, in that year your total tax (on both the sale and your other income) will exceed the sales price of the property. You should be prepared for this when the time comes.

If I can be of further help please let me know.

Exhibit 6-2: Analysis of Tax Shelter Investment

Wilson Weir
Comparison of tax effects of investment in
Tax Shelter Partnership No. 1

Year	Investment	Tax Loss	Excess Dep'n	Accumulated excess Dep'n	Tax Without the Investment	Tax With the Investment	Decrease in Income Tax
(1)	$ 26,000	$ 59,834	$ 7,482	$ 7,482	$ 27,086	$ 1,870	$ 25,216
(2)	26,000	68,182	11,234	18,716	30,040	1,337	28,703
(3)	26,000	37,386	4,922	23,638	33,181	14,488	18,693
(4)	26,000	38,474	494	24,132	36,520	17,283	19,237
(5)	—	7,896	(1,500)	22,632	40,069	36,121	3,948
(6)	—	5,300	(1,960)	20,672	43,841	41,191	2,650
(7)	—	2,342	(1,446)	19,226	47,852	46,681	1,171
(8)	—	832	(1,324)	17,902	52,115	51,699	416
(9)	—	190	(1,716)	16,186	56,646	56,551	95
(10)	$ 104,000	$ 220,436	$ 16,186		$ 367,350	$ 267,221	$ 100,129

Sale in tenth year for $104,000

					Tax Without the Investment	Tax With the Investment	Decrease in Income Tax
Line (10) above					$ 367,350	$ 267,221	$ 100,129
Tax in tenth year					61,463	110,406	(48,943)
					$ 428,813	$ 377,627	$ 51,186

NOTE: This exhibit reflects tax losses in excess of the amounts invested or at risk. Under tax law in effect when this was written real estate is the only investment where deductible losses can exceed the amount at risk.

For limited partners in other types of investments the losses will be limited to amounts invested or at risk. Further, there will be 100% recapture of depreciation in year of sale.

Exhibit 6-2: Analysis of Tax Shelter Investment (Continued)

7

The Pros and Cons
of Professional Corporations

In recent years the professional corporation has become important in tax planning for members of all professions. This has been a slow process which has overcome imposing obstacles. For many years state laws prohibited professionals from practicing in corporate form. Gradually a concept of professional liability within a corporate framework emerged, and state legislatures passed laws permitting professional corporations to be organized. In the meantime the Internal Revenue Service was negative on professional corporations, creating a number of uncertainties that have been overcome with the passage of time.

Members of professions are now permitted to incorporate throughout the country, the Internal Revenue Service now recognizes these entities, and most of the uncertainties have been resolved. Professional corporations are now used widely and effectively to provide significant tax and financial benefits.

This chapter offers guidance in all aspects of providing tax and accounting service to the professional corporation.

10 KEY FACTORS TO CONSIDER BEFORE INCORPORATING

1. The Structure in Which the Client Practices. Some professional practices can operate successfully with a corporation and some can't. The first consideration, therefore, is the environment of the practice and how well it can adapt to incorporation.

Generally the larger the organization the more problems there are to be overcome. A large partnership, for example, has established procedures for compensating partners, for determining the amount of each partners' capital, and for determining amounts to be paid to partners upon withdrawal for retirement.

A partnership permits flexibility in these arrangements that is sometimes difficult to achieve in the more structured environment of a corporation. Generally, the more partners in the practice and the more complex the financial arrangements between partners, the more difficult it will be to solve the problems of incorporating.

A small partnership, even one with two partners, can run into problems when looking at incorporation. This generally comes about where there is a disparity between the ages of the partners. The older partner has different retirement objectives and needs for immediate cash compensation than the younger partner. In addition, it may be easier to work out an arrangement for the younger partner to buy out the older in a partnership than in a corporation.

The history of the partnership should be reviewed. How long have the partners been together? Do they enjoy a compatible, stable relationship? Is there a record of professionals leaving the firm? Incorporation should be considered only by those practitioners who expect to stay together for many years.

To sum up, incorporation is not for everyone. The accountant should assume responsibility for looking at the practice environment to determine if a professional corporation is practical and in the client's best interest.

2. Variations in Corporate Group Practice Arrangements. Some professionals associate themselves in a group practice that is primarily for sharing overhead or office expenses rather than a true partnership. Each professional's earnings are based primarily on his own production, out of which he contributes to the common expenses shared by the group.

If such a group wants to incorporate it will be necessary to examine whether they should set up one corporation for the entire group, or whether separate corporations should be used for each practitioner. Separate corporations provide more flexibility and would appear to be more workable. A problem to be resolved is the treatment of common employees who are not employed by one of the corporations. If these employees were not covered for retirement purposes the IRS might withhold approval of the corporate retirement plans of the members of the group.

A similar arrangement is a partnership made up of several professional corporations as partners. This arrangement is set up for two reasons: each professional has his own corporation and can set up a retirement plan to his liking; the common employees of the partnership are not covered under any corporate retirement plan, thus saving that expense to the members. Such an arrangement is questionable from the standpoint of whether the IRS will approve the corporate retirement plans.

The accountant needs to be able to advise clients concerning these and other possible arrangements of corporations.

3. Financial Discipline of a Corporation. A professional corporation makes significant changes in the way finances are handled—the corporation imposes more financial discipline than does a partnership. In most cases this is beneficial and is one reason for recommending incorporation. Some professional clients, however, do not want this type of financial discipline imposed on them. The client should be fully informed that a corporation will require him to go on a salary with income tax withheld, that the corporation cannot pay his personal bills, etc. If he is unwilling or unable to operate in this environment he should not incorporate.

In some instances the financial discipline alone is sufficient reason for incorporating. In our practice we have seen instances of professionals whose finances have improved significantly simply because of going on a salary and paying income tax through withholding. Whereas the client had previously struggled to pay his income tax each year (having to borrow money because he had already spent everything), after incorporating he found he was able to live on his salary after income tax was withheld.

4. The Professional Client Investor. Some professional clients love to wheel and deal—they are continuously involved in various types of investments. Careful consideration should be given as to whether this kind of client should incorporate.

Some clients are the entrepreneurial type with a knack for making good investments, and enjoy doing so; they may be better off without a corporation. They have more flexibility in using their resources and may prefer to pursue investments rather than to contribute to a retirement fund. If this method works for them, they should stay with it and not incorporate.

Some professionals, on the other hand, are not good investors. Most of their investments are those on which they have been sold, either as a fantastic opportunity or a tremendous tax shelter. Such a client relies on others for investment advice and makes investments that often turn out poorly. Such a client would be better off with the financial discipline of a corporation. His or her income tax would be paid through withholding and he or she would contribute as much as possible toward retirement. Investments would be limited to funds available after payment of taxes, retirement, and living expenses.

5. Tax-Saving Considerations. If the client seems to be a suitable candidate for incorporation, the next step is to determine the tax advantages. Although there are other benefits from incorporating, tax saving is the primary motivation. The tax advantages are in the following areas:

- A corporate retirement plan that provides benefits beyond those available through a Keogh plan.

- Tax-deductible group hospital and life insurance coverage not available to the self-employed.

- In some cases, availability of a medical reimbursement plan (where appropriate coverage is offered other employees).

- Lower corporate income tax rates where it is necessary to build up capital in the practice.

Each client will have to be considered on his individual merits to determine which benefits are the most practical or advantageous. At the top of the list in all cases, however, is the adoption of a corporate retirement plan. This is the primary reason for incorporating in virtually every case. A professional corporation is probably not worth the effort if the client is not willing to go into larger retirement contributions than afforded by a Keogh plan.

In some instances a professional practice will require sufficient capital to make it advantageous to build up capital at corporate income tax rates. In other cases, the financial discipline imposed by a corporation is a significant advantage. In the vast majority of cases, however, the decision on incorporating can be directly related to the corporate retirement plan.

Don't overlook the potential tax increases that come with a corporation. These include additional payroll taxes on the professional's salary (compared with self-employment tax) and any state and local taxes incurred by corporations. While these are generally relatively minor items, they should be considered and the client made aware of them.

The tax advantages must be carefully worked out by the accountant and communicated to the client. This is done by providing comparisons of the tax position before and after incorporation. The results should be provided to the client in writing as well as reviewed orally. An example of these comparisons is found in Exhibit 7-1.

When reviewing the tax savings with clients, it is important to point out that this is actually a tax deferral—not a permanent saving. Tell the clients about having taxable income when they receive their retirement benefits—and about taxable income that may come when the corporation is dissolved or when they sell their stock.

All presentations of tax information and accounting data should be given in a simple, straightforward manner. Most nonaccountants have trouble following accounting and tax figures and terminology, and appreciate a presentation that is easily understandable.

6. Corporate Retirement Plan Considerations. When reviewing the tax savings afforded by a corporate retirement plan, it is necessary to also review with the client the various types of plans available. This matter is closely related to the decision to incorporate, and a clear understanding of the type of plan that will be adopted is essential.

In this and other aspects of professional incorporation, the accountant should suggest bringing in other professional advisers where appropriate. The client's attorney will, of course, be involved and bank trust officers, life insurance company representatives, and others may be needed.

In discussing corporate retirement plans the accountant should give the client an understanding of the difference between a "defined contribution plan" and a "defined benefit plan." The client must understand the advantages and disadvantages of each to make a basic decision about which way to go.

There are instances where a defined benefit plan is difficult to use because of age disparity between the professionals in the practice. The contribution to fund a defined benefit for the older practitioner is much greater than for the younger. This disparity can be overcome by adjusting the salaries of the members to offset the disparity in the retirement contribution. Setting up a defined benefit plan is more complex where there are several practitioners to be considered.

A defined benefit plan, however, should not be rejected without serious consideration. This type of plan affords opportunities for substantial retirement contributions, particularly for older professionals. Every effort should be made to work out the problems so that maximum tax benefits can be obtained.

In discussions at this stage the objective is simply to give the client an idea of the different kinds of plans available, and the amounts that can reasonably be put into retirement. It is not necessary before incorporation to make final decisions, but for the client to get an understanding of where he or she is heading.

7. Professional Liability. One consideration the client should review is any change in the legal status of his or her professional liability. State laws differ in this respect, but some, if not all, states limit liability to the shareholder performing a negligent act (the professional is responsible for his or her own acts but not those of others). The accountant should defer advice in this area to the client's attorney, but should suggest that the matter be considered.

8. Management. Professionals in group practice may find the corporate management structure advantageous. With corporate officers and a board of directors, the responsibility for management functions may be more clearly structured than in a partnership. The process of incorporation will require the professionals to consider business aspects of the practice that may have been neglected in a partnership. Further, the need for annual meetings of shareholders and directors is helpful in stimulating periodic reviews of business and financial matters.

9. Continuity of Life. A corporation will continue in existence indefinitely unless it is dissolved or its charter forfeited. Its existence is not affected by death, termination of employment, bankruptcy of a shareholder, etc. This feature is an advantage over the partnership form and should be pointed out to the client.

10. Transferability of Ownership. The transfer of shares of corporate stock is a simpler, more clear-cut transaction than is the transfer of a partnership interest. Furthermore, the shares of stock may be divided into different classes having certain preferences and limitations, such as voting and nonvoting stock.

SETTING UP THE CORPORATION

Once the client and his or her advisors have determined that a professional corporation is workable and advantageous the next job is to get it set up and underway. The accountant has an important part to play throughout this process.

1. Initial Investment and Capital Structure. Most professional corporations can be set up without the complications involved in larger corporations. The majority of professional practices have modest capital requirements and the problems of thin capitalization, debt vs. equity, etc., are not present.

The corporation is usually started when a proprietorship or partnership decides to incorporate. The assets of the existing practice are transferred to the corporation in a tax-free exchange under IRC Section 351. If the client has been reporting on the cash basis for tax purposes, his or her receivables have no tax basis and are not a factor in the amount of stock to be issued. Stock is issued only for those assets having basis, and these normally consist of cash and equipment used in the practice. Unless these amounts are large, the corporation should issue only stock in exchange for them. If there is a large amount of equipment, consideration can be given to issuing a combination of stock and debentures. The amount of cash transferred to the corporation should be only that which is required for current operations.

It is unwise to transfer accounts payable to the corporation if the taxpayer is on the cash basis. The payables should be paid by the predecessor organization, since it incurred them. The only liabilities transferred to the corporation should be notes payable on equipment being transferred or similar items.

It is now generally recognized that receivables of cash basis taxpayers can be transferred to the corporation at a zero tax basis. As they are collected they will be recognized as income by the corporation. In the early stages of the professional corporation concept there was concern that the IRS might not permit recognition of this income by the corporation, but this problem seems to have been resolved.

The accountant should close the books of the predecessor proprietorship or partnership and determine the assets and liabilities to be transferred, their tax basis, and the amount of stock to be issued. This information should be transmitted to the client and his attorney in writing so that everyone has the same information (see letter in Exhibit 7-2).

2. Setting the Initial Salaries. An important point to be worked out at this stage is setting the salaries of the professionals. This will be a new experience for them, not having been on a salary before. It is important to get them off on the right foot at the very outset.

The initial salary should be set at an amount that will, after tax withholding, provide for the current living expenses of the client. The salary figure should also be related to the expected annual corporate income, less retirement contribution. The salary should, therefore, fall within these criteria:

- Meet the living expenses of the client
- Not be so high that it creates working capital problems for the corporation
- Not be so low that it leaves excessive cash in the corporation
- Be set at a realistic level that will lend itself to reasonable annual increases in the future (but not drastic increases)

It is normal to declare a bonus for the client at the end of the corporate year, so that any increase in earnings during the year can be paid to him or her at that time.

3. The Employment Agreement. During the initial salary discussions the need for an employment agreement should be brought up. A written agreement that spells out the employment arrangements helps put the corporate setup on a solid footing. The agreement should state the initial salary and provide that annual increases will be determined by the board of directors. An annual bonus should be provided in the agreement. Duties, responsibilities, vacations, fringe benefits, and the like should also be covered.

A corporation with more than one professional member should have a provision for disability in its employment agreement. Agreement should be reached on continuing compensation of the disabled member, the need for insurance coverage, and what happens if the disabled member cannot return to work. The accountant should see that this important matter is not overlooked.

4. The Buy-Sell Agreement. A corporation with more than one professional member should have also have a buy-sell agreement. When such an agreement is lacking the unexpected death of a shareholder puts extra stress on everyone, both the remaining shareholders and the decedent's family, to negotiate the purchase of his or her interest. It is much better to have the terms spelled out in an agreement that eliminates the need for negotiation after death.

The buy-sell agreement will also come into play when a shareholder decides to retire or to withdraw from the corporation. Again, a carefully spelled out agreement negotiated in advance makes such a separation much easier to accomplish.

The accountant probably has more experience in these matters than anyone else, should recommend that such agreements be prepared, and should advise on various provisions.

5. How to Handle Buildings and Equipment. The practitioner who owns his own building should retain ownership in his name and lease it to the corporation. This is preferable to transferring the property to the corporation, for several reasons:

- The building is an investment asset, and such assets should not be in the corporation.

- The equity in the building will increase as it is paid off, and this equity should not be in the corporation.

- If the building has large interest and depreciation expense there may be a loss for tax purposes, which is best used on the personal return.

- The building will probably appreciate in value and this appreciation should not be in the corporation.

Some accountants recommend that the equipment be held individually and leased to the corporation. While an argument can be made for this, it is not nearly as strong as in the case of the building. The equipment is not an investment asset and it generally does not appreciate in value. The important factors that dictate holding the building out of the corporation, therefore, are not present with equipment. Further, items of equipment are continually being added or replaced, requiring a continuous adjustment of the rent and creating administrative and bookkeeping problems. These problems may be aggravated where several practitioners are involved.

For these reasons most accountants recommend having the corporation own the equipment. Exceptions can be made, however, where the facts warrant.

CLIENT WHO INCORPORATES MUST OPERATE LIKE A CORPORATION

The most important point the accountant can make to the client who wants a corporation is this: if you want the benefits of a corporation, you must operate like a corporation! To do otherwise invites IRS problems that could be serious indeed.

Many practitioners with experience in this area, including the writer, know of cases where the client has formed a corporation without legal assistance, failed to open a corporate bank account, failed to set up a salary for himself or herself, continued to use his or her individual IRS employer identification number, and the like.

The accountant's first responsibility is to steer the client away from these pitfalls. In our firm, we write to newly incorporated professional clients, outlining a comprehensive list of points that must be complied with (see Exhibit 7-3). A copy of this letter also goes to the client's attorney. The letter is supplemented with discussions regarding various points that must be emphasized, particularly regarding salaries and bonus arrangements, retirement plans, and the like.

Several basic points should be made to the client and are listed below for emphasis:

- An attorney should set up the corporation, prepare the bylaws, and assist with the organizational meeting.
- A written employment agreement should be set up for the professional at the very beginning, spelling out salary and bonus arrangements.
- Corporate minutes must be kept up to date.
- A corporate bank account must be opened.
- Personal transactions must not be run through the corporation account.
- The corporation must do all payroll tax reporting in its own name, obtaining its own identification number from IRS.
- A board of directors must be elected and function in accordance with state law.
- The corporate name must be used at all times.

Failure to take care of these matters at the beginning will usually result in a scramble to straighten out and redo things at year end. It is dangerous for the accountant to become involved in such activities, and it is in his interest and the client's to do things right from the beginning.

A professional corporation has significant benefits, but to enjoy those benefits it is necessary to operate like a corporation.

SERVING THE ONGOING NEEDS OF THE CORPORATE CLIENT

Adoption of a Corporate Retirement Plan

Once the corporation is underway and the accountant is satisfied the client understands how he should be operating, attention should be turned to the corporate retirement plan. A decision must be made during the first corporate year concerning adoption of a plan. The process should begin early enough in the year so the client has plenty of time to consider alternatives.

The accountant should explain to the client that he has several choices to consider:

- He can adopt a defined benefit plan or a defined contribution plan.
- He can adopt a plan that includes life insurance benefits, or can exclude life insurance.
- He can adopt a plan wherein he is appointed as trustee, or can elect to use an outside trustee.

The client who wants to thoroughly consider all these alternatives will most likely need to discuss the programs available through bank trust departments, life insurance companies, and savings and loan associations. The client should review as many alternatives as possible within the limits of time available for this purpose. The client should recognize the importance of setting up a program to take care of his or her retirement and that of the employees, and should allocate as much time as is needed to explore all avenues.

The accountant should be available to counsel with the client to the extent needed in this process. Some clients will make a decision quickly and some will take considerable time. Some will discuss the program with the accountant thoroughly and some will not. The accountant should be available to do what is necessary to help the client, but most important, should see that a decision is made before the end of the corporation's first tax year and necessary papers are signed.

If the client chooses an "independent" plan, where he serves as his own trustee and no prototype master plan is involved, the plan and the trust instrument will have to be prepared for the client. He should, incidentally, be informed that this cost will be incurred when he decides to follow this course.

The trust instrument should be prepared by the client's attorney. The plan itself, however, can be prepared by an accountant who is knowledgeable in the retirement plan field. The accountant who assumes responsibility for a professional client practice must, indeed, become proficient regarding retirement plans. He can properly service his professional client only if he is skilled in IRS requirements regarding employee coverage, vesting provisions, reporting requirements, etc. The accountant should assume responsibility for preparing the profit sharing or pension plan, counseling with the client regarding various provisions where choices must be made; get the plan completed within the required time frame, submit it to the IRS for approval; and follow through on IRS mandated changes to see that final approval is forthcoming.

The accountant should also plan to assume responsibility for seeing that the annual IRS reporting requirements are met and that the annual accounting is prepared for employee allocations.

If the plan is operated through an insurance company or other outside entity the annual accounting and reporting may be handled by them. The responsibility for this should be clearly established, and the accountant should be prepared to do this work if necessary. This is an area that can be neglected or overlooked to the detriment of the client, and the accountant should be sure this does not happen.

Current Accounting and Financial Statement Needs

The newly incorporated professional client must be made to understand that a professional corporation requires better accounting than does a proprietorship. Responsibility for preparation of the accounting records should be fixed—either with the client's bookkeeper or with the accountant's office. If the client's personnel are to be responsible, it is advisable that the accountant review the accounting periodically during the year.

It is advisable that financial statements be prepared on a monthly or quarterly basis. The client and the accountant need to see how the corporation is doing as the year progresses.

Annual Review Prior to Year End

Planning for the year end is critical to the success of the professional corporation—and must take place in advance. Most professional corporations have characteristics that make this advance planning essential:

- The corporation is a cash basis taxpayer.
- A decision must be made prior to year end as to the amount of earnings to pay out in year-end bonuses and the amount to leave in the corporation as retained earnings.

The normal practice for many professional corporations is to pay out substantially all earnings each year in the form of bonuses and contributions to the retirement plan. While retirement contributions can be paid within two and one half months after year end, bonuses of a cash basis taxpayer must be paid *prior* to year end. This latter requirement makes advance planning essential.

The procedure followed by our firm is to obtain the client's ledger during the last month of the fiscal year and review the figures for the first eleven months. This gives a good picture of the year-end tax situation and permits some tentative conclusions as to bonuses and retirement contributions. Before making any final decisions, however, it will be necessary to get some idea of what will happen during the twelfth month. *This is necessary before the end of the month.* About a week before year end the client should provide income and expense figures for the twelfth month to date, and an estimate of the last few days. With this information, the necessary computations can be made as to the bonuses and retirement contributions.

It should be remembered that the retirement contribution is based on the total compensation, including bonuses. The two figures are interdependent and must be so computed. An example of the type of computation used by our firm is shown in Exhibit 7-4.

Pitfalls to Avoid in Operating the Corporation

The operation of a professional corporation is not a static thing; new problems and challenges are continually arising for the accountant because of ideas clients get or practices they adopt.

Some clients see money accumulating in the corporation during the year and can't resist the temptation to take advances. One of the purposes of getting periodic financial statements is to make the client and the accountant aware of this practice, and the extent of it. We have seen cases in our firm of clients who have taken advances during the year and then been shocked at year end at the total amount taken.

If the client's advances become too large there may not be sufficient funds to pay the retirement contribution, or to pay necessary income tax withholding on the bonus declared to cover the advance. It is possible to declare a bonus, but not have sufficient cash to pay the proper income tax withholding. This leaves the client owing tax on his personal return, and he may have to take another advance to pay his tax.

To avoid these problems one or more of the following recommendations can be made:

- Compute bonuses on a quarterly basis, pay the bonus and appropriate income tax quarterly (this reduces the temptation to draw advances).

- Put any extra corporate funds into a savings account until year end (get it out of the checking account so the client won't be so likely to notice it).

- Discourage advances, but recommend that if an advance is necessary, sufficient funds be put into savings to cover the income tax payment that will be due when the bonus is determined.

Another problem arises with the client who resists paying himself a bonus that will be taxed at 50%, preferring to leave the money in the corporation at lower tax rates. This client is frequently coming up with ideas about how the corporation can invest its excess funds. In our firm, for example, we have observed that clients interested in real estate investments find the idea of having the corporation buy real estate an attractive alternative to pulling out bonuses at a 50% personal tax rate. For the reasons set out below we always strongly recommend against making investments with corporate funds.

The client must be reminded of the initial reason for incorporating—to get the benefit of a corporate retirement plan. It is customary to withdraw most of the annual corporate earnings through retirement contributions and bonuses. Earnings normally are retained in a sufficient amount to provide working capital. It is generally best to limit the use of the corporation to conducting the professional practice and building up a good retirement fund.

The client should be urged to avoid making investments with corporate funds. He or she should be advised to make investments with personal funds. If the corporation makes a poor investment and suffers a capital loss it is difficult for the corporation to deduct the loss. On the other hand, a successful investment can result in having assets in the corporation that the stockholders will have difficulty getting out without declaring a dividend.

Retaining Earnings to Buy Out a Stockholder

There is an exception to the general rule of retaining only sufficient earnings in the corporation for working capital needs. If a stockholder is planning to retire in the foreseeable future the corporation should consider retaining funds for the purpose of buying his or her stock. These funds can be accumulated at lower corporate tax rates, followed by a redemption of the stock at capital gain rates. The combined corporate rate and capital gain rate will be likely to result in an overall tax saving as compared with distributing the income currently as a bonus.

Accumulating earnings for the purpose of getting funds to a stockholder at capital gain rates can also work with one stockholder. Corporate earnings distributed to a stockholder upon liquidation can result in long-term capital gain at that time.

A personal service corporation can accumulate up to $150,000 of retained earnings without IRS challenge for unreasonable accumulation of earnings.

Such a program should be entered into only when there is a well-thought-out plan for a stockholder to retire. The accumulation of earnings should be held in a type of investment so that the funds will be available when needed to buy the stock or liquidate the corporation.

	Initials	Date
Prepared By		
Approved By		

ANALYSIS OF BENEFITS OF INCORPORATING

Green and Gould
Analysis of tax benefits of incorporating

LINE NO			No Retirement Plan	HR 10 Retirement Plan	Corporate Retirement Plan	LINE NO
1	Net income — partnership		270000	270000	270000	1
2						2
3	Partnership distributions: Green		110000	93000		3
4	Gould		110000	93000		4
5						5
6	HR 10 contributions: Green			13950		6
7	Gould			13950		7
8	Employees			6100		8
9						9
10	Corporate salaries: Green				85000	10
11	Gould				85000	11
12						12
13	Corporate retirement contributions:					13
14	Green				21000	14
15	Gould				21000	15
16	Employees				8000	16
17			270000	270000	270000	17
18						18
19	(continued)					19

Exhibit 7-1: Analysis of Benefits of Incorporating

	Initial	Date
Prepared by		
Approved By		

LINE NO	(1)	(2) No Retirement Plan	(3) HR10 Retirement Plan	(4) Corporate Retirement Plan	LINE NO
1	Income from partnership or Corporation	110000	93000	85000	1
2	Itemized deductions & exemptions	15000	15000	15000	2
3	Taxable income	95000	78000	70000	3
4	Federal income tax	31790	23934	20414	4
5	Net after tax	63210	54066	49586	5
6	Add retirement benefit		13950	21000	6
7	Total economic earnings	63210	68016	70586	7
8					8
9	HR 10 advantage		4806		9
10	Corporate advantage			7375	10
11					11
12	Cash flow comparison				12
13	Income from partnership or corporation	110000	93000	85000	13
14	Less income tax	31790	23934	20414	14
15	Cash available	78210	69066	64586	15
16					16
17	Reduction in cash available: HR10 Plan		9144		17
18	Corporation			13624	18

Exhibit 7-1: Analysis of Benefits of Incorporating (Continued)

Mr. Fred Williams
Attorney-at-Law
Brownsville, Texas 78520

Dear Fred:

The books for Green and Gould (partnership) have been closed and the following assets have been transferred to Green and Gould, P.C.:

Cash		$ 11,000.00
Equipment	$64,509.59	
Accumulated depreciation	41,845.59	22,664.00
		$ 33,664.00

I understand the authorized stock is 50,000 shares of $1.00 par value. I recommend that 16,832 shares each be issued to James Green and Larry Gould in exchange for the above assets.

No liabilities were transferred to the corporation.

I suggest that the corporate minutes reflect that these assets were transferred to the corporation in exchange for stock in a transaction qualifying as a tax-free exchange under Section 351 of the Internal Revenue Code.

If you need anything else from me give me a call.

CSCjr:mz
cc: Green and Gould, P.C.

Exhibit 7-2: Letter to Attorney Regarding Transfer of Assets and Issue of
Stock

Messrs. James Green and Larry Gould
Brownsville, Texas 78520

Dear James and Larry:

This is written for the purpose of outlining various points regarding operation of your professional corporation. The items listed cover various characteristics of corporate activities and should be carefully followed. If any doubt arises as to whether a particular procedure should be followed or changed, please ask for advice *in advance*:

1. A corporate bank account should be opened with sufficient operating capital to meet your needs.

2. All office supplies including stationery, patient ledger cards, patient records, business cards and any other documents involving governmental agencies or the general public should bear the correct name of the corporation. If you intend to continue using old supplies make certain that the corporate name is somehow reflected on the items being used.

3. You will become an employee of the corporation. Income tax and social security taxes must be withheld from your salary, employee earnings records maintained, and proper reporting made to the Internal Revenue Service and Texas Employment Commission.

4. Accurate records should be maintained on all business expenses incurred by the corporation. This is particularly applicable for travel, entertainment, automobile, and convention expenses. All expenses should be paid by corporate check with proper explanation and documentation.

5. The corporate name should be reflected on the door of your office.

6. The corporate name should be listed in the telephone directory, together with any listings with professional societies, associations, and so forth. Your status as a professional corporation should be known to your colleagues.

7. All insurance policies such as workmen's compensation, physical damage on furniture, fixtures and equipment, malpractice, owner's, landlord and tenant liability, group hospital, etc., should be assigned to and owned by the corporation.

8. All leases for office space or equipment should be assigned to and reflect the corporation as lessee.

9. Any professional fees for legal services, accounting or tax advice, insurance advice, and investment and management advice should be paid through the corporation.

10. Your salary initially should be set realistically and should not vary substantially from year to year. It is normal to increase salaries as practice income increases but large fluctuations should be avoided.

11. Your corporation will close its fiscal year on August 31. A corporation income tax return will be prepared by us for filing each year by November 15.

Exhibit 7-3: Letter to Officers of New Corporation

12. The new federal identification number for the corporation should be used on all IRS documents and forms.

13. Have all state licenses transferred, if necessary.

14. Payables should be paid by you up to date of incorporation. Notify all creditors to bill you in the corporate name after January 1.

15. All receipts from patients coming in after January 1 should be deposited to the corporate bank account.

16. *Never* pay any personal items from the corporate bank account.

17. The corporation can reimburse you for business use of your automobile. You should determine a specified monthly allowance and adjust it periodically as conditions change.

18. The corporation can provide group life insurance coverage for its officers and employees. You can each be covered up to $50,000 tax free to you. This should be discussed further with an insurance agent.

19. The corporation can adopt a retirement plan covering you and other eligible employees. *This is the most important tax benefit of* incorporating. When your are ready to consider this we can discuss the various types of plans available.

This list is not intended to be all-inclusive, but simply a guide regarding various important points.

If you have any questions please give me a call.

CSCjr:mz
cc: Mr. Fred Williams, attorney

Exhibit 7-3: Letter to Officers of New Corporation (Continued)

Green and Gould, P.C.
Year end tax planning projection
for fiscal year ending August 31

		1	2	3	
1	Profit through July - cash basis			83000	1
2					2
3	Projected collections - August		41000		3
4	Projected expenses - August		36000	6000	4
5					5
6	Projected cash profit			89000	6
7	Depreciation for the year			17000	7
8	Projected profit before bonuses and retirement			77000	8
9					9
10	Bonuses			30000	10
11				47000	11
12	Projected retirement contributions :				12
13	Green and Gould		30000		13
14	Other employees		8000	38000	14
15					15
16	Projected corporate taxable income			9000	16
17					17
18					18
19					19
20	FOR CASH BASIS CORPORATIONS THESE COMPUTATIONS MUST				20
21	BE MADE BEFORE YEAR-END.				21

Exhibit 7-4: Year-End Tax Planning Projection

8

Helping the Professional
with General Business Advice

A BROAD CONCEPT OF THE ACCOUNTANT'S ROLE

The opening paragraphs of Chapter 1 discussed the need for the accountant to think in broad terms about the services he can give professional clients. The successful accountant thinks of the total economic well-being of the client and contributes to it in a variety of ways. Most professional clients feel the need for a broad range of services and are willing to pay for them. (See Exhibit 1-1 for a survey of health care professionals regarding their present use of CPSs and their needs for expanded service).

This chapter discusses the specifics of general business advice, a fascinating field of service whose scope and variety is indeed wide—and limited only by the innovation and expertise of the accountant.

HELPING THE NEW PRACTITIONER GET STARTED

The beginning practitioner poses a challenge to the accountant and provides an opportunity for rendering much needed service. This professional in some respects has more need for service than does his experienced counterpart, but on the other hand may not realize it.

The matter of how much service the beginning practitioner can afford must be considered. The accountant may spend considerable time and end up with a sizable bill. The initial accounting fees, however, should be looked upon as an investment by the beginning practitioner—one that is necessary to get a practice off on the right foot.

The accountant who services the new client attentively and thoroughly will have a loyal, satisfied client for many years—and will experience the good feeling of a job well done.

There are many areas where the experienced accountant can advise a young professional client. The discussion that follows outlines as many potential areas of service as possible. The accountant obviously will not provide all these services to any one client, but may have an opportunity to provide them to various clients over a period of time.

The particular services rendered will depend on the client's need and the accountant-client relationship. Some clients will have other persons with whom they discuss problems, while some will rely heavily on the accountant because he or she is the most accessible, knowledgeable adviser around.

Services Relating to Philosophy of Practice

The beginning practitioner should develop a philosophy of practice in the early stages of his career. The accountant, as an experienced professional, can assist the client in developing such a philosophy. The accountant has undoubtedly considered this matter in connection with his own practice and career, and can discuss it with his client in a meaningful way, helping him think through the various aspects of the problem.

The accountant can help the client consider the type of practice he wants to develop, reviewing the pros and cons of the following:

Developing a large practice over a period of years, bringing in associates and building up a staff to accommodate a substantial clientele.

Limiting the size of the practice to work the practitioner can perform individually, permitting him to handle carefully selected clients who will receive personal attention and quality service.

Practicing in a specialized area, either within an individual practice or within a larger organization.

The philosophy of practice also encompasses the concept of professionalism. The accountant can use his experience to help the beginning professional client in this area. The client needs to be clear in his objectives regarding public service, rendering service to certain groups gratis or at a reduced fee, and the like. This ties in with the philosophy that a professional practice is different from a commercial business, in that rendering professional service is the primary objective, followed secondarily by the profit motive.

The accountant also may have an opportunity to discuss with the client the need for staying abreast of current developments, for keeping up-to-date. All professions are finding their fields of knowledge to be continually changing and expanding, and every professional must keep up-to-date. If the accountant feels his client has a tendency to become complacent he may be able to motivate him to keep up-to-date.

Be sure the client is aware of the changing environment in which members of all professions practice. Pressures from consumer groups, Federal agencies, and the courts have caused significant changes in professional rules regarding advertising, solicitation and competitive bidding. This will directly affect the way in which the client conducts his practice, and of equal importance, will affect the action of his competitors. The professional client should be clear on the current status of these matters as it affects his profession.

Gaining Initial Recognition and Contacts

The new practitioner may need assistance in getting acquainted and getting established in the community. It is possible he might look to his accountant, as a professional who has been through the same problem, for guidance. There are numerous ways to accomplish this, and the accountant can discuss those that seem appropriate:

Increasing acquaintances by becoming active in community organizations, particularly serving in capacities where one's professional expertise can be put to use.

Making contacts with other members of the same profession with a view to assisting overburdened practitioners and/or obtaining referrals.

Considering the use of advertising, which is now permitted by most if not all professions (this discussion should include consideration of whether advertising is an effective way to promote a professional practice).

Encouraging the client to be prepared to accept speaking engagements before appropriate groups.

Encouraging the client to write for publication, both locally or in professional journals—writing brings recognition to the practitioner from professional colleagues and from clients.

Discussions with the client should emphasize that the most effective method of building a practice is providing first class service. First class service makes for satisfied clients who invariably provide word-of-mouth advertising. While the methods mentioned above can be effective in the right circumstances, client service is by far the most important practice-building tool.

Indoctrinating the Beginning Client in Financial Matters

The accountant will undoubtedly advise the beginning client in financial matters—a subject directly related to the accountant's field of expertise. This is an area where the new practitioner can run into problems—particularly someone who has little background or training in financial matters. Young professionals who start a practice and enjoy immediate financial success frequently do a poor job of handling their finances. Several areas where the accountant can serve the client are discussed below.

Finding the Right Banker and Lawyer

Professionals starting their own practices should start off right with expert advice and assistance in areas where they need it most—accounting, legal, and banking matters. If you, as the accountant, are the first professional employed by the new client, you can help by steering him or her to a good lawyer and a good banker.

In recommending a lawyer, point toward someone who will take the time required to properly serve the client, who will relate to the needs of a young, inexperienced professional, and who provides prompt service. Try to stay away from someone who is habitually behind in his work and slow in getting things done, or who is obviously too busy to properly take care of the clients he already has. It is clearly best to use a lawyer who deals primarily in business matters, as opposed to a trial lawyer, who is difficult to reach and concentrates on courtroom matters.

In recommending a banker, you need to consider whether to recommend a specific individual or a specific bank. This, of course, depends on the circumstances in each individual case, and will have to be decided accordingly. Individual bankers tend to move around and for that reason it might be preferable to recommend a bank that would suit the client's needs, then choose a banker within the bank.

Some banks cater to professional clients by setting up departments trained to service the professional group. This is a factor in considering which bank to recommend, but the primary consideration is actual performance. In some banks one or more officers will have become familiar with the banking needs of professionals simply by working with them. The accountant serving professional clients should be aware of these capabilities and be able to inform his or her clients of them.

Helping the Client Arrange Financing

Helping the client arrange financing is closely tied to recommendation of a banker. The client should have a banker who understands the needs of professional clients and can relate to them. Some professionals have little need for capital, while others, such as dentists, have a considerable investment in equipment. Some professionals, such as lawyers and architects, sometimes have jobs or cases that continue for extended periods of time before income is received, creating a need to finance working capital by loans.

The beginning practitioner may not fully understand the financial requirements of his or her practice, or the need for financing. The accountant should work with him or her in preparation of cash flow projections and financing requirements. This service is similar to that rendered a commercial client, but is tailored to the particular financial requirements of the professional and is related to the needs of the practice. The financing requirements of the practice may cover purchase of initial equipment or working capital needs while the practice income is building up.

An illustration of such a projection is found in Exhibit 8-1.

Advice to the client regarding financial needs covers not only how much he needs to borrow, but where to go for financing. The accountant should advise as to alternate sources of funds, and the pros and cons of each.

Most professionals can arrange bank financing if they choose to do so, since professional clients are generally rated a good risk by banks. In most instances bank financing is probably better than other sources, but all sources should be evaluated.

A dentist setting up shop will purchase considerable equipment and the equipment manufacturer is usually in a position to arrange financing. The local bank may also be willing to finance equipment, in which case an evaluation must be made as to which route to follow. Interest rate and credit terms should be considered, as well as such intangibles as the value of doing business with a local bank, which lender would be the most reasonable to deal with in case of problems, personal relations with the banker, and the likehood of becoming better known and establishing a credit rating locally.

An illustration of an analysis of financing alternatives is found in Exhibit 8-2.

Management of Personal Finances

An important area of working with new professional practitioners is the handling of personal finances, including how much to withdraw from the practice in the form of a salary or a drawing account. This subject will be discussed thoroughly in Chapter 10, "Working With Professional Clients on Financial Management and Goals."

Helping the New Practitioner with Office Location and Equipment

The inexperienced professional just getting started can benefit from advice from an experienced accountant regarding setting up an office—location, equipment, and how much to spend initially.

Location. Location depends on the type of profession and the type of practice to be developed; a trial lawyer needs an office near the courthouse, for example. Some practitioners have a great deal of office traffic and should be easily accessible, both by private and public transportation. Others need an office near the commercial and financial center of the city. Some will want to consider accessibility and parking for both clients and office staff. Some have staff members leaving the office to work at other locations, making easy access an important point.

Another factor to be considered is the trend and direction of population growth in the community. Information should be obtained from a knowledgeable source, such as the Chamber of Commerce, regarding these trends. For some professionals an office location in a growing area of the community can be most advantageous.

A study should be made, also, of the location of the competition—other practitioners in the community. The beginning practitioner can then decide whether it is better to be located near the competition or to find a location in a different area.

The accountant, who is familiar with the community, can discuss the pros and cons of various locations with the client, helping him think through some of the alternatives before making his decision.

Most beginning practitioners will lease rather than buy their office facilities. The cost of leasing office premises is, therefore, a major consideration in setting up shop. The accountant is probably more knowledgeable about leasing costs and various leasing arrangements than the client. If the client has looked into several locations he may have proposals with varying provisions regarding such matters as who pays utilities, janitor service, initial office improvement and renovation costs, and what items of space are included in computing square footage for rental purposes. The accountant can help the client evaluate the financial aspect of all these variables. (See Exhibit 8-3).

Office Equipment. Considerations when equipping the office: (1) how much equipment is needed; (2) whether to lease or buy, or some combination thereof; (3) if financing is needed, how to arrange it.

The accountant can guide clients as to how much equipment is needed—particularly cautioning them against going overboard. Most professionals setting up practice will be well advised to acquire only what is absolutely necessary initially. Additional equipment can be added later. Some find it hard to resist the temptation to buy everything available, which may be more than they can afford initially. For example, computers keep coming down in cost and manufacturers devise programs to fill every need. A computer is probably a luxury, however, that the beginning practitioner can afford to get along without for awhile.

The matter of furnishing the office can present difficult choices. A professional office should present an image of permanence and success. This image can be achieved at varying levels of cost, and the beginning practitioner again may need to resist the temptation to go overboard. Luxuries in the form of expensive furniture, oil paintings, and the like are not needed initially—indeed, they might create an adverse reaction from clients at the outset. Such luxuries can be added later as the practice prospers.

Helping the New Practitioner Set Fees

The setting of fees is an area where the accountant is experienced and can help the new client. Each profession has its own methods of setting fees and the accountant must be knowledgeable regarding each profession.

Most practitioners increase their fees regularly throughout their professional careers. There are several reasons for this:

As the practioner develops more expertise and experience his services become more valuable to the client.

A successful professional attracts a larger clientele as the years go by—his services are more in demand and he is justified in charging more.

The professional works for larger clients or on larger jobs, assuming more responsibility, therefore commanding a higher fee.

Fees must be increased to keep up with inflation.

The accountant can help the new practitioner in determining fees initially, and in determining when to increase fees. It is necessary to set them at a level that will cover all costs and provide a reasonable profit.

The timing of fee increases will depend on the level of inflation, the demand for the client's service, the economic conditions in the area, and other factors. Any timing of fee increases should be set to minimize client resistance, and consideration should be given to the time of year and other factors that might affect this.

It is advisable to discuss the need for communication with clients or patients about fees. The primary factor in a satisfactory fee relationship with the client is that he should not be surprised. If a fee will be high, the client should be advised in advance. The accountant should strongly urge his professional client that good communication is essential to a good client relationship regarding fees.

Helping the New Professional with Office and Personnel Procedures

One area where the accountant can offer his services is in assisting the beginning professional client in setting up office and personnel procedures. This subject was covered in Chapter 2, "Helping Your Client Manage His Office and Improve His Accounting System."

HELPING THE EXPERIENCED PRACTITIONER WITH ONGOING PRACTICE PROBLEMS

The accountant will find that most of his dealings with professional clients are with experienced practitioners who are coping with the ongoing problems of running a practice—building a sound financial base while faced with high taxes, expenses, and living costs, finding the demands on their time increasing year by year, and generally dealing with the stresses of life in a professional environment.

Dealing with the experienced professional covers a wide range of areas that are discussed throughout this book. This particular discussion centers on general business areas of advice and assistance not covered elsewhere.

Control of Productivity and Workload

One of the challenges faced by any successful professional is that of controlling his time, productivity, and workload. The demands and pressures of a practice can grow to the point that the professional is totally immersed in his work, to the exclusion of other aspects of his life. Affirmative action is required to bring the workload and time pressures under control so the practitioner doesn't become a workaholic and does have time available to lead a balanced life, including leisure, travel, vacations, and hobbies. Indeed, the more successful professionals are those who have found the key to productivity—they fulfill their professional responsibilities within a reasonable time span and have sufficient time away from the practice for other activities.

Accountants themselves have to cope with this problem, understand the factors involved, and can, therefore, help their professional clients deal with it.

An accountant who is close to his professional client can see if the client is becoming a workaholic or seems to be less productive. This is evidenced by long working hours, little or no time for outside activities, and a financial return that is low in relation to the responsibilites assumed and the hours worked.

Once the accountant recognizes the problem, the next step is to find a way to bring it to the client's attention. This will depend on the accountant-client relationship and the nature of the individuals involved. Indeed, some professionals undoubtedly enjoy being totally immersed in their work and have no desire to change. Other clients, however, may not be conscious of their situation and would welcome constructive assistance.

The accountant may have mastered certain technqiues in managing his own time or in learning to delegate work to others, and may feel that what he has learned would be helpful to the client. He should, therefore, make an effort to assist in whatever manner is best suited to the situation.

Management of time. The ability to manage time effectively has come to be recognized as a subject of major interest to all professionals. It is the subject of numerous seminars and books. Both the accountant and the professional client have opportunites to explore the subject in depth. The following is a brief listing of points the accountant could cover with the client when discussing this subject.

Scheduling The professional's schedule should provide separate blocks of time for different major activities. Some time should be scheduled to permit uninterrupted work. The professional should arrange his schedule so that he is in control of it rather than being controlled by others.

Start and finish a job. Every effort should be made to keep pending unfinished items to a minimum. Once a job is started, it should be brought to a conclusion—stay with it until it is finished. A large number of unfinished assignments makes it difficult to work in an orderly manner.

Limit accessibility. A professional must be accessible to clients and staff. Clients don't look with favor on a professional they can't reach when they need him. Accessibility must, however, be subject to certain limits. Certain times of the day should be set aside to deal with clients and with staff, and certain times should be free of interruption.

Selectivity of clientele. The experienced practitioner must learn to limit his clientele. The demands on his time will not permit serving the same clientele he did in his early years of practice. He must concentrate on larger clients or on those problems within the area of expertise he has chosen. It is sometimes difficult for the practitioner to recognize the need to take this step. He may not want to offend clients or potential clients by being selective, but a successful professional must eventually do so.

Learning to Delegate to, and Rely on, Others

The art of delegating to, and relying on, others is in reality a part of the subject of management of time, but it is discussed separately because of its importance.

Professional practitioners must anticipate that their work will change as their career progresses. Not only will the type of clientele change, as discussed above, but in most professions they must learn to continually delegate and rely more on the work of others. Most professionals will find that eventually they will spend most of their time reviewing and supervising the work of others, rather than doing it themselves. The ability to do this, therefore, will directly affect the growth and productivity of the practitioner.

Here are several areas where the accountant can help a professional client to learn the art of delegation.

Use of a secretary. A skilled and dedicated secretary can be the most valuable asset the professional has. The secretary can arrange the schedule, control the flow of traffic, handle routine telephone calls and other communications, and generally make the practitioner more productive. The accountant can advise the client on specific ways to use a secretary. The talents and personality of the secretary are important, as is the secretary's ability to work with the practitioner. Increasing benefits flow from this arrangement after experience is gained in working together.

Use of professional associates. The practitioner should consider employing less experienced associates to perform the routine work he did himself in earlier days. The nature of the work will vary in different professions, but every experienced practitioner should be able to delegate work to others. Some are reluctant to do so because of long-standing client relations, a fear that no one else can do the job, etc. The accountant may be able to rely on his own experience to convince the client that delegation is feasible and has many advantages.

Use of paraprofessional associates. The use of paraprofessionals is increasing in most professions. As the cost of professional services continues to increase, a continuing effort is underway to find more efficient and economical ways to perform the work. It has been found that much can be accomplished by a trained paraprofessional, and at a cost below that of a full professional. The accountant should see, therefore, that his professional client is aware of the possibilities of using paraprofessional talents.

Keeping up with New Developments and Technology

The professional client in the course of his career may become lax in keeping up with new developments and technology. If the accountant has a close working relationship with the client he may be able to recognize this and attempt to do something about it.

The accountant should be aware of new developments and technology through his own practice and association with other clients. He should urge his professional clients to stay abreast of changes and developments in a number of areas:

A major development affecting all professions is new computer technology. The use of computers comes into play in many aspects of professional practice. Some of these are familiar to the accountant and some are beyond his sphere of knowledge. He should urge his clients in all cases to keep up with this changing area in order to utilize the latest methods in their practices and take advantage of equipment and procedures that will make their work more efficient.

The accountant should be aware of the latest developments in office technology, such as word processing equipment, and advise his clients when use of such equipment seems appropriate.

Professional clients should be urged to participate in activities of their profession, particularly taking time to attend seminars and keep up-to-date.

Preparation for the unexpected. Unexpected developments occur in the personal and professional life of a client, such as divorce, disability, lawsuits, even death. The accountant can make his client aware of the possibility of these events and of the need to be prepared to cope with them. Some areas where assistance and advice can be offered are as follows:

Practice continuation. The continuation of the practice in event of disability should be considered. The sole practitioner is particularly vulnerable since his practice could dissipate quickly. He should, if possible, have a practice continuation agreement with another member of his profession. Those in group practice should have an agreement with their colleagues providing for suitable compensation for their share of the practice in case of death or disability (see Chapter 9 for further discussion).

Insurance requirements. The accountant can see that the client is aware of the basic types of insurance coverage and carries as much as needed:

Workmen's compensation insurance
Premises liability insurance
Building and equipment casualty insurance
Office overhead insurance in case of disability
Business interruption insurance
Malpractice insurance
Umbrella insurance

Divorce. The divorce of a professional client has many financial ramifications and the accountant frequently becomes involved. If the client has financial responsibility for a family he will become obligated for child care support. He will also be concerned with a property settlement or alimony payments to the ex-wife. All this puts a substantial strain on the client's income and assets. The accountant can help the client evaluate the financial effect of the divorce and plan for his financial future. He may also be called upon by both parties to provide information concerning income and assets (he may, in fact, be the one party in whom everyone has confidence, since divorces sometimes result in hard feelings and mistrust). An important role of the accountant is to point out the tax implications of the proposed divorce settlement. The parties to a divorce, and their lawyers, frequently overlook the tax effect, and the accountant should insist on reviewing the settlement prior to its execution and point out tax problems.

CONCLUSION

General business advice is indeed a broad field. The accountant who is skilled in working with clients in this area will find himself engaged in many interesting, varied assignments. Such work is professionally satisfying, financially rewarding and sets the accountant apart as a person who can do more than prepare financial statements and tax returns.

JOHN KENT, D. D. S.
PROJECTION OF CASH FLOW REQUIREMENTS
For First Year of Practice

	First Quarter	Second Quarter	Third Quarter	Fourth Quarter	Full Year
Cash Receipts					
Capital invested	$ 10,000	$	$	$	$ 10,000
Gross receipts from patients	25,000	30,000	35,000	50,000	140,000
	35,000	30,000	35,000	50,000	150,000
Cash Disbursements					
Fixed expenses:					
Salaries	9,000	10,000	10,000	12,000	41,000
Rent and utilities	3,000	3,000	3,000	3,000	12,000
Dues and subscriptions	250	250	250	250	1,000
Insurance	2,000	500	250	250	3,000
Laundry and uniforms	300	300	300	300	1,200
Legal and accounting	600	400	400	600	2,000
Professional education	500	500	500	500	2,000
Taxes	1,250	1,250	1,250	1,250	5,000
Telephone	150	150	150	150	600
Variable expenses:					
Outside lab work	4,000	6,000	7,000	8,000	25,000
Dental supplies	3,000	2,000	2,000	2,000	9,000
Office supplies	2,000	500	500	1,000	4,000
Business promotion	500	500	500	500	2,000
Allowance for unforeseen and unidentified expenses	3,000	2,500	2,500	2,000	10,000
	29,550	27,850	28,600	31,800	117,800
CASH FLOW BEFORE PERSONAL WITHDRAWALS	5,450	2,150	6,400	18,200	32,200
Personal withdrawals	6,000	6,000	6,000	6,000	24,000
CASH FLOW BEFORE DEBT RETIREMENT	$(550)	$(3,850)	$ 400	$ 12,200	$ 8,200

Exhibit 8-1: Projection of Cash Flow Requirements

JOHN KENT, D. D. S.
ANALYSIS OF ALTERNATIVE FINANCING ARRANGEMENTS

	First National Bank		Dental Equipment Credit Corporation
	Alternative No. 1	Alternative No. 2	
Amount of loan	$ 45,000	$ 45,000	$ 45,000
Interest rate	14%	14%	16%
Term of loan	See A	See B	See C
Monthly payments	$ 1,047	$ 1,047	$ 834
Total payments of principal and interest	$ 62,820	$ 69,120	$ 80,064

A Sixty level monthly payments starting immediately.

B. Interest paid only at end of first twelve months followed by sixty level monthly payments.

C Ninety-six level monthly payments starting immediately.

ANALAYSIS OF ADVANTAGES AND DISADVANTAGES OF EACH PROPOSAL

First National Bank—Alternative No. 1

Advantages:
  Lower interest rate.
  Lower total cash outlay.
  Enhances establishment of local credit.
  In case of problems, permits dealing with local institution.

Disadvantages
  Shorter term loan and higher monthly payments.

First National Bank—Alternative No. 2

Advantages:
  Lower payments during first twelve months while practice is building up.

Disadvantages:
  Larger total outlay than Alternative No. 1.

Dental Equipment Credit Corporation

Advantages:
  Longer term loan and lower monthly payments.

Exhibit 8-2: Analysis of Alternative Financing Arrangements

Disadvantages:
   Larger total outlay than other alternatives.
   Dealing with an out-of-town corporate lender, in which case it might be more difficult if there is a problem.

<u>Recommendation</u>

   The analysis of alternative financing arrangements must be studied in conjunction with the first year cash flow projection (Exhibit 8-1).
   Cash flow projected for the first nine months of practice will not support monthly amortization of debt. In fact, it appears that personal withdrawals will be difficult to achieve during the first six months. The third quarter shows a modest improvement, followed by a dramatic cash flow increase during the fourth quarter.
   The financing arrangement that fits this situation best is Alternative No. 2 of the First National Bank. Under this alternative there will be no payments of principal or interest until the end of twelve months, when the first year's interest will be due. Your cash flow projection indicates funds will be available to pay the annual interest of $6,300 at the end of twelve months. Further, you should be able to meet the monthly payments of $1,047 without difficulty beginning in the second year.
   There are other advantages to using a local financial institution, as mentioned above under the advantages and disadvantages of the alternatives.
   We recommend, therefore, Alternative No. 2 of the First National Bank.

Exhibit 8-2: Analysis of Alternative Financing Arrangements (Continued)

JOHN KENT, D. D. S.
ANALYSIS OF ALTERNATIVE LEASING ARRANGEMENTS

	Mayfair Plaza	Coronado Building
Cost of leasehold improvements to be paid by you	$ 9,000	$ 11,000
Monthly rental	$ 1,400	$ 1,800
Utilities	400	included
Janitor service	100	included
Monthly cost	$ 1,900	$ 1,800
Annual cost—rent, utilities, janitor service	$ 22,800	$ 21,600
Amortization of leasehold improvements, five year life		
Annual amortization	1,800	2,200
Total Annual Cost	$ 24,600	$ 23,800

The accountant can, if appropriate, analyze factors such as location, quality of the premises, ability to expand space, if needed, and other similar considerations.

Exhibit 8-3: Analysis of Alternative Leasing Arrangements

9

Helping the Professional Client with Problems of Group Practice

Dr. Atlas has been your client since she set up practice eight years ago. You have worked with her closely and have watched her practice grow. You have a good relationship and have provided substantial assistance in business and tax matters.

She now tells you she wants to seriously consider bringing in an associate, and wants your advice. She knows you are experienced in this area, both through dealing with other professional clients and as a partner yourself in an accounting firm.

SERVING CLIENTS BEYOND TAXES AND ACCOUNTING

The above discussion depicts a typical situation where the accountant is given an opportunity to serve his professional client beyond the usual tax and accounting areas. Guiding the client in getting into and operating a group practice is a natural field of service for the accountant—one where his expertise in taxes, accounting, and general business matters can all be put to effective use.

Participation in group practice by professionals is an important decision—one in which numerous factors must be considered. The paragraphs below discuss many of these factors, alerting the reader to points that should be considered when advising clients in this area.

Five Advantages of Group Practice

The client who asks your advice regarding group practice is probably already aware of certain advantages, but may not have considered all the benefits stemming from association with others.

1. Ability to Offer a Wide Range of Services. All professions are experiencing a knowledge explosion which makes it impossible for one person to offer in-depth knowledge in all areas of practice. Group practice permits the members to specialize in chosen areas; varying specialties provide the vehicle for offering a wide range of services.

2. Resources to Utilize Enlarged Staff and Equipment. Several practitioners joining together have resources to enhance their staff and facilities—to employ assistants and technicians, to acquire equipment, to expand the library.

3. Consultation with Others. A professional needs to be able to discuss problems with his peers. A practitioner who has no one to talk problems over with is indeed unfortunate. Group practice provides the opportunity for discussion and consultation—a significant advantage of this method of operation.

4. Sharing of Responsibility. The professional can feel more comfortable going away on vacation or attending meetings if someone is handling his responsibilities at the office. In group practice the members share responsibilites and help each other out—creating the good feeling that the entire burden of the practice isn't on one person's shoulders.

5. Continuity of Practice. In most professions an ongoing professional practice has considerable value—but this value can dissipate upon death or disability of the practitioner. This threat is overcome by group practice, particularly when there is a well-thought-out written agreement covering the purchase of the interest of a withdrawing, retiring, or deceased member.

Getting Started in Group Practice

The accountant may be called upon to advise clients who are putting a group together for the first time, or to advise a sole practitioner who is considering joining an existing group. While the thrust of the advice may vary in these two situations, there are many common pitfalls to avoid and points to consider carefully.

A group practice constitutes a professional marriage and should be thoroughly thought through before signing on the dotted line—those who haven't done this all too often end up with a professional divorce. Some of the more important factors to consider are discussed below.

Careful selection of members. It should hardly be necessary to mention the obvious point about careful selection of members—but some groups are formed without enough consideration of certain important factors.

- The members should have professional goals and objectives that are in harmony. They should get to know each other well, and learn enough of each other's background to be sure they are headed in the same direction.

- The members should understand that group practice requires each, to some extent, to put the good of the group ahead of his personal desires. A person unwilling to do this is not a good candidate for group practice.

Type of Organization Structure to Use. The members will have to decide whether to use a partnership or a professional corporation. As discussed in Chapter 7, the principal reason for going into a professional corporation is to set up a corporate retirement plan. A group just getting started probably shouldn't get involved in a retirement plan immediately (there are other more pressing matters to work on first) but still should consider incorporating, for several reasons.

- If a group starts off as a corporation, the problem of changing over later from a partnership is avoided. Some practitioners get accustomed to the partnership operation and are reluctant to switch to a corporation later. Use of a corporation at the beginning avoids this problem.

- A corporation permits the purchase and sale of shares of stock, which is generally considered less complex than buying and selling a partnership interest.

- A corporation will probably place a limit on professional liability (in some states an incorporated professional is fully liable for his own negligence but not for that of the other members).

- A corporation requires certain formalities and financial discipline that are good for the group. Each member, for example, is required to go on a salary, eliminating potential partnership problems that could arise by partners drawing whatever funds are available. The corporate form requires election of officers and holding of meetings, a form of organizational discipline that may be advantageous.

A professional corporation is not for everyone, however; some groups find the flexibility and less formal requirements of a partnership fit their needs better.

The accountant advising clients in this area should ask probing questions to be sure he understands the goals and objectives of the members sufficiently to help them make the right decision.

Need for Written Agreement Covering All Contingencies. Some groups talk over their plans, build up a lot of enthusiasm, then simply shake hands and go to work. Clients should be strongly advised against making a firm commitment until all aspects of the deal have been thoroughly discussed and the entire agreement put in writing by an attorney.

HELPING WITH ONGOING OPERATING PROBLEMS

Understanding the Need for Management Authority

Clients in group practice need to understand that they have created an organization which requires continuing management attention. Group practices vary greatly in size and, therefore, management problems will differ accordingly. However, any group of two or more professionals will need to reach an understanding concerning management responsibility.

One member of the group should assume management authority and responsibility. An organization doesn't function well with several people in charge. It is generally a mistake for everyone to take a hand in management—or to attempt to divide it up among the members.

In some groups none of the members are particularly interested in assuming management responsibilities. Some have attempted to resolve this problem by rotating the manager's job—passing it around among the members on a rotating basis. This will probably lead to poor results. Each member will be likely to consider the job a burden and fail to give it sufficient attention. A group in this situation should consider employing a manager who devotes the proper time and attention to the job.

A medium-sized to large group should look at the advantages of hiring an administrative manager. The manager would be a person trained in management, not in the profession itself. This person can save the professionals considerable time by assuming administrative details. This position should be structured so that the manager is accountable to one or more members of the group, and is not given unlimited authority.

The Important Matter of Sharing Earnings

One of the most important matters to be decided by the group is how to share earnings—how to "cut the pie." The arrangement for this will vary with different professions, but certain principles are applicable to all.

The simplest approach is to share the net earnings equally. Many groups start with such an arrangement. This system may work for awhile, but often it will become apparent that certain members are contributing more than others, and dissatisfaction will result.

In some professions a workable arrangement is one where each member's earnings are related to his or her own production—that is, expenses are shared equally and income is shared based on production. This system is considered by some to be oversimplified, however, resulting in development of more sophisticated approaches.

Some groups use a formula that borrows that best of both systems—one that its proponents say allocates both income and expenses fairly under varying circumstances. The formula works like this:

Gross income - the first 25 percent is divided equally among all members; the remaining 75 percent is divided according to the productivity of each member.

Expenses - fixed expenses are divided equally among the members; variable expenses are divided among the members according to the productivity of each.

The reasoning behind this formula is that each member derives the majority of his income from his own productivity, but shares a portion equally on the theory that the group as a whole is responsible for at least a part of each member's success. If a member wants to take an extra-long vacation, for example, the primary impact is on his own earnings, or if he is not doing as well as he thinks he should, he can become more productive and enhance his earnings.

The theory behind the two categories of expenses is that if one member is seeing more patients or clients than the other he is also making more use of supplies, office staff, etc., and should be charged accordingly. Also, if one member takes a month's vacation he is still charged for his share of the fixed expenses.

It can be readily seen that this formula introduces some careful cost accounting, an area where the services of the accountant become important. Discussions must be held with the members to determine which expenses should go into the fixed category and which are considered variable. In working this out, it is not necessary to strictly follow the usual cost accounting principles—the members should be free to allocate expenses between the two categories in any way they feel best suits their purpose.

Another variation is to divide the income in the following manner:

50 percent of the gross income is distributed according to the number of patients each member saw as a percentage of the total seen by the entire group.

The other 50 percent is distributed according to the dollar charges put on the books by each member as a percentage of total dollar charges of the group.

This formula is considered a fair way to divide earnings among members with different specialities. For example, a surgeon sees a limited number of patients but his charges per patient are high compared to those of a pediatrician, who sees many patients but has a lower charge per patient. In deciding to allocate income on the formula described above, or some variation of it, the members must determine the relative importance of seeing a large number of patients as compared to dollar charges put on the books.

Not all professions can use the formula described above. While the productivity of each member is important in all professions, the measurement of such productivity and the methods of sharing earnings must be handled differently.

One procedure used rather widely is to share earnings according to the number of units held by each member. Additional units are awarded periodically, based on an evaluation of each member's contribution to the group. Each member is awarded additional units (an important psychological factor) but the more productive members are awarded more than others. The factors to be considered in awarding units are productivity, management responsibilities, and ability to bring in new business.

It is immediately obvious that for this system to work a management structure must be in place that has the respect and confidence of the members. The awarding of units is a subjective matter that must be handled with great care and diplomacy. Frequently a certain amount of negotiation is required to settle the number of units for each member. The members must be convinced that everyone is getting fair treatment and that they are better off than they would be elsewhere.

The process of evaluating members and determining the units to be awarded should be initiated by the managing partner. If he has the respect of the members he may handle this task entirely on his own. One other approach is to use a small committee of members for the job—an effective procedure in a larger group.

There should be an agreement as to the frequency with which additional units will be awarded. An annual award is generally the most effective and the most widely used procedure. Others go on a biannual or triannual basis. Each member should be aware of the time at which units will be awarded and the process should be faithfully followed as agreed.

Withdrawals of Earnings by Members

Members in a group must follow an agreed procedure as to withdrawal of earnings. A policy that is fair to all must be set up and enforced. Members should not be permitted to make extra withdrawals or advances except in case of emergency and upon approval of the managing partner.

Withdrawals should be made on a regular basis to cover the current living expenses of the members. This is in the nature of a salary, even though it may actually be a withdrawal of earnings. Extra withdrawals, or bonuses, should be distributed as funds are available, but again on a regular schedule.

Members in a professional corporation will receive salaries, with bonuses distributed periodically. The schedule for bonuses will depend on the circumstances, but should relate to such factors as the need to have money available for income tax and other purposes. The income tax requirement will largely be taken care of, however, by withholding.

A partnership has no income tax withholding from the withdrawals of the members, who will be paying estimated tax on a quarterly basis. The extra withdrawal schedule, therefore, should consider the income tax requirements of the partners. Some partnerships distribute extra withdrawals only at estimated tax payment dates to be sure members have funds available for this purpose.

Clients entering group practice should be advised that control of withdrawals is essential to the success of the group practice. A group where members draw money at random, with some members drawing more than their share, runs a real risk of dissension.

Loss of Income due to Wrongful Acts of a Member

The agreement of some groups provides that a member can be charged with the amount of reduced earnings caused by his own wrongful acts. A provision of this type is found in Exhibit 9-1.

It seem abundantly clear that such a provision should be used sparingly and in only the more serious instances. The group may prefer to part company with a member who has committed a wrongful act of sufficient magnitude to bring such a provision into play.

Life Insurance Coverage

The group should be advised to consider life insurance coverage on the members. Such coverage provides needed financial assistance in the event of death of a member, similar to key man life insurance for commercial corporate clients. Insurance proceeds would be used for these purposes:

- Providing funds to make up for lost revenue due to death of a member
- Providing funds to pay the obligation to buy out a member's interest after his death

The accountant can assist the group in evaluating insurance proposals, particularly in regard to the use of term or whole life coverage. Most professional associations provide group life insurance coverage at attractive rates and the accountant should be sure the group considers this alternative.

How to Deal with Incapacity of a Member

The group should recognize the possibility that a member may become incapacitated either temporarily or permanently. This can present a serious problem, particularly if provisions have not been made in advance for handling the situation. The agreement should spell out what will be done, with particular concern that any payments to the disabled member are reasonable and fair, both to the incapacitated member and to the rest of the group.

Exhibit 9-2 presents an example of an agreement providing that an incapacitated member shall continue to receive his share of earnings for the first six months. He will continue as a partner in the firm for an additional six months, receiving only his regular withdrawal, which is charged to his capital account (no share of earnings after the first six months). The remaining partners may request the withdrawal of the incapacitated partner after one year of disability, or may grant a leave of absence of an additional twelve months. This provides, therefore, that a member may remain with the group for twenty-four months if the other members agree. This would, of course, depend on the prognosis for recovery.

ACCOUNTING AND REPORTING REQUIREMENTS OF THE GROUP

Need for Current, Reliable Financial Data

Many of the points discussed previously in this chapter can be put into effective use only with good accounting records. The accounting system of the group must provide current, reliable data, and may need considerable sophistication. If income of the members is related to their own productivity, for example, the system for measuring productivity must have the confidence of the members.

At a minimum, the accounting system should provide the following:

- Double-entry general ledger accounting for all assets, liabilities, income, and expenses.
- Current operating statements and statements of financial position.
- Accounting for accounts receivable, with an updated list given each member.

The members will probably want additional data in the way of operating statistics. The accountant should be closely involved in developing the system for this.

Need for Members' Confidence in Accounting

The members must be confident that the accounting data is reliable and the system is operating for the benefit of all concerned. The accountant can play an integral part in assuring that this is the case. There are a number of ways in which he can participate in the accounting and reporting process, serving as an objective, outside party who is working for the entire group.

- If the group has its own accounting staff which prepares accounting records and reports, the accountant can perform an annual audit. In some groups the managing partner insists on an audit to assure the other members that the financial reports are reliable. The subject of auditing professional clients is fully discussed in Chapter 5.

- In many instances the accountant may be employed to perform the service of preparing accounting records and financial statements. This service provides assurance to the members (although not to the extent of an audit) and usually results in more reliable accounting than the group would get from their own staff.

- Some groups have the accountant take substantial control of their finances by paying bills and signing checks in addition to keeping the books. This type of service is used in some cases where it is felt an outsider should perform these functions so that no one member of the group exercises undue influence on the accounting process.

HANDLING WITHDRAWAL OR RETIREMENT OF A MEMBER

An important consideration in group practice is making provision for withdrawal or retirement of a member of the group. When advising clients on group practice the accountant should be sure this matter is not overlooked. Practitioners who are inexperienced in group practice sometimes ignore this problem; they are concerned primarily with current operating problems and figure they will handle withdrawal or retirement later.

The group should be strongly advised to have their agreement put in writing by an experienced attorney, including provisions for withdrawal or retirement. The agreement should be specific as to the responsibilities and benefits accruing to a member in this situation.

One of the benefits of group practice is that of having withdrawal or retirement benefits agreed upon and the assurance of receiving this benefit. It is much more likely that this will be handled properly if the terms are put in writing. On the other hand, failure to do so can be the cause of significant problems upon withdrawal, retirement, or death of a member.

Payments to Withdrawing Member

The practice of various professions differs a great deal, causing variations in payments to withdrawing members of groups. In some professions there is a strong personal relationship between the individual practitioner and the patient or client, with limited loyalty to the organization. Goodwill, therefore, is not a significant factor in these instances.

In other professions the organization is the key factor and clients tend to stay with it regardless of the departure of individual members. In this situation payment for this goodwill is customary upon departure of a member.

The amount to be paid a departing member must be fair to both parties—an amount all concerned feel is reasonable for the interest being purchased. This may be calculated as a percentage of the fee volume of client responsibility given up, as measure of the net income of the departing member, or as a subjective payment for past services rendered.

Payment terms must be such that the remaining members can handle the payments without seriously affecting their own income. Payments are generally made monthly and constitute a retirement benefit to the departing member. Some groups have an agreement that the aggregate payments being made to departed members cannot exceed a certain percentage of gross revenues.

Tax Treatment of Payments to Departing Members

Payments to departing members generally consist of several components, the tax treatment of each of which should be carefully considered. The various components and their tax treatment are described below.

- *Reimbursement for capital invested.* In all cases the capital invested by the member will be returned to him, either in the form of paying off his partnership capital account or purchasing his corporate stock. The tax treatment is that accorded any purchase and sale of a partnership interest or capital stock.

- *Share of accounts receivable and work in progress.* The departing member will probably be entitled to his share of accounts receivable and work in progress existing at time of his departure. These amounts are ordinary income to the member and deductible in full by the group.

- *Payment for goodwill or past services rendered.* Any payments in excess of capital invested, accounts receivable and work in progress will have to be considered as either for goodwill or for past services rendered. The tax treatment of such payments is quite important, and is discussed in the following paragraphs.

If payments to a departing member are considered to be for goodwill the group will have a nondeductible capital expenditure and the payee will have a long-term capital gain. If the payments, on the other hand, are for the past services rendered, the group will have a deductible expense and the payee will have ordinary income.

A group that plans to continue in existence for a long period of time can ill afford to buy out one or more members with payments that are not deductible for tax purposes. The remaining members are very likely in a high tax bracket and should not be making nondeductible payments.

If the payments are considered to be for past services rendered, the departing member will have ordinary income. If he has retired, however, he may be in a lower tax bracket than his former colleagues who are still active.

In most cases the best economic result for all concerned is obtained by classifying the payments as for past services rendered. The accountant should, therefore, advise clients to be very careful in structuring the agreement regarding these payments, and to avoid setting up purchase of goodwill unless there are strong reasons for doing so.

It is important that all members are in agreement on the treatment of such payments for tax purposes. If the parties are in agreement and treat the payments accordingly on their tax returns it is unlikely that the Internal Revenue Service will challenge the arrangement.

Exhibit 9-3 provides an example of a method of determining amounts due for past services rendered.

One word of caution: payments for past services by a professional corporation could be questioned if the departing member has not previously worked for the corporation. For example:

Able, Baker and Charlie have practiced together as a partnership for years. Able decides to retire and is entitled to receive compensation for past services rendered. Immediately after Able's retirment Baker and Charlie form a professional corporation, which continues to pay the agreed amount for past services. It is possible that the IRS might challenge the deductibility of these payments by the corporation on the ground that Able was never employed by the corporation.

Expulsion of a Member

The group should have a provision in its agreement stating that a member can be expelled. The possibility must be recognized that a member may become unsuitable for a number of reasons and the relationship terminated. The agreement should specify that the other members may, by unanimous vote, expel a member, and further, that a member automatically ceases to be a part of the group in certain specified situations, such as:

- Loss of license to practice in the profession
- Personal bankruptcy

An example of a provision for expulsion of a member is found in Exhibit 9-4.

CONCLUSION

Group practice has many advantages and is the way most professionals practice. A group encounters many accounting, tax, and operating problems with which the accountant can deal effectively. Helping the professional client with the problems of group practice is, indeed, a rewarding and satisfying service.

Wrongful Acts

The above division formula notwithstanding, the amount by which net earnings of this partnership are reduced or the amount of any net operating loss incurred by this partnership as a result of the wrongful acts, willful or gross negligence, dishonesty or fraud of a partner shall be first charged to the offending partner before any allocation is made of net earnings or losses. The right of determining what constitutes a wrongful act under this Article shall rest with the partners other than the offending partner.

Exhibit 9-1: Provision Regarding Charging a Member for Loss of
Earnings

Participation

In the event any partner becomes completely unable to perform his duties as a partner by reason of illness, accident, or other causes, he shall continue to receive his share of profits for a period of six (6) months. Should the period of complete disability extend for a period longer than six (6) months, his share of profits shall then cease, but he shall continue as a partner for an additional six (6) months over the above initial six (6) month period. During the second six (6) month period the partner shall be paid his normal monthly drawing account, which amounts will be charged to his capital account.

Income Protection Insurance

Each partner is encouraged to carry income protection and disability insurance to provide for himself. The partnership shall pay for and charge to the respective partner's drawing account income protection or disability insurance premiums.

Leave of Absence

The remaining partners may, in their discretion, after the passing of the first twelve (12) months of incapacity, grant a leave of absence of not more than one (1) year to such incapacitated partner. Such partner is not to participate in profits during the period of his leave of absence.

Withdrawal of Incapacitated Partner

The remaining partners may at any time after a partner has been incapacitated for a continuous period of more than one (1) year request such incapacitated partner to withdraw from the partnership upon the same terms as provided under Article 5 (Death of Partner).

Medical Certification

The disabled partner shall, upon requests of the other partners, provide appropriate medical certification as to his complete inability to perform his duties as a partner.

Exhibit 9-2: Provision Regarding Incapacity of a Member

ADDITIONAL AMOUNTS DUE DECEASED, INCAPACITATED, WITHDRAWING, EXPELLED, OR RETIRING PARTNERS

It is recognized that each partner contributes to the ongoing value of the firm through his abilities and efforts over the years; therefore, partners leaving the service of the firm are entitled to additional compensation for the past service of the firm under provisions of Articles 5, 6, 7, 8 and 9, and are entitled to compensation for said past services according to the following formula:

Years of service as a partner:	Entitled to the following percentage of his individual earnings during the highest two out of the five full years immediately preceding the date of leaving service:
30 years or more	100%
Over 25 but less than 30 years	80%
Over 20 but less than 25 years	65%
Over 15 but less than 20 years	50%
Over 10 but less than 15 years	35%
Over 5 but less than 10 years	20%
Less than 5 years	-0-

In case of withdrawal between the five-year dates enumerated above, the percentage to which the withdrawing partner is entitled will be determined by a pro rata allocation of the specified percentages.

Total Years of Service

A partner's years of service include those years as a partner in the existing firm, plus years in any predecessor to this firm and any other firms which have merged into this firm.

Exhibit 9-3: Provision for Determining Amounts Due Departing
Member

Right to Expel

A partner may be expelled from the partnership at any time by a unanimous vote of all other partners.

Notice Required

A partner shall be given thirty (30) days' written notice of his expulsion before it shall take place.

Effect of Expulsion

The expulsion of a partner shall have no effect upon the continuance of a partnership, and the remaining partners shall have the right to continue the partnership business.

Terms of Expulsion

Upon expulsion, the interest of the expelled partner shall be paid for accordingly to the provisions of Article 7.3, 7.4, 7.5, and 7.6

Exhibit 9-4: Provision for Expulsion of a Member

Working With Professional Clients on Personal Financial Planning

There are several ways to describe the services discussed in this chapter:

- Personal financial counseling
- Family financial planning
- Financial goal setting

Whatever the description, the objective is the same: to help the client in the important area of handling personal finances wisely and building a sound financial base.

SETTING FINANCIAL GOALS

Professionals spend years learning the skills of their work. Many earn a handsome income. Yet many have limited knowledge of finances, letting too much of their earnings slip away through poor spending practices or unwise investments.

The key to financial success lies in planning and setting goals. The clients must know what they want to accomplish financially. It is imperative that they have the right advice.

The professional client has the opportunity to obtain advice from a variety of individuals. Many are selling on a commission basis and some, therefore, may not be completely objective in their advice.

The client needs an objective adviser; one who does not derive income from the investment decision, who can analyze the pros and cons of the proposed investment and who will not let his personal preferences affect his advice. The accountant is well suited for this role. He has a solid financial background and experience. He is employed by the client and paid by the client. He has regular contact with the client and is familiar with his financial situation. The accountant should, therefore, be a key financial adviser.

Financial counseling and planning encompasses many aspects of the client's affairs:

- Personal budgeting and control of expenses

- Management of debt, both personal and investment related
- Planning for investment opportunities
- Insurance programs
- Retirement planning
- Estate planning

An important point to bear in mind: financial planning must involve the direct participation of the client. The accountant should avoid making decisions for the client, always staying in an advisory capacity. The client should be urged to take the time to learn, listen, read, and inform himself—and to participate in discussions with his accountant regarding financial planning and investment decisions.

Establishing Specific Financial Goals

Inflation and high taxes have combined to make it more and more difficult to get ahead financially. This applies particularly to professionals, whose main source of income is taxed at ordinary income rates in high tax brackets. The need to build up a substantial net worth to offset the decrease in purchasing power is particularly important for the professional client.

At the outset of financial counseling with the client, the accountant should lead the discussion into areas of financial goals the client should consider. Several of these are basic and should be of concern to all clients.

1. Need for emergency funds. A requirement in every financial plan is a savings account to be kept intact for use in event of serious illness and other emergencies. Such a fund should contain a minimum of three to six months' income.

2. Education of children. A basic financial responsibility is the education of children. Planning for this should begin as early as possible. There are several approaches to accumulating these funds:

- A systematic savings plan for this purpose
- Diverting investment income to children (see discussion of ten year trusts in Chapter 6)
- Building a financial base that will take of the need when the time comes

3. Retirement. For the majority of clients an important element of retirement planning will be the use of a qualified profit sharing or pension plan. The use of these plans is discussed in Chapters 6 and 7. The client who participates in a tax-deductible retirement plan has taken a major step in accumulating retirement funds. It may be desirable to go further, however. Consideration should be given to the need for additional funds and how these will be accumulated. Many points made elsewhere in this chapter will help achieve comfortable retirement status.

4. Achieving financial independence. Clients differ greatly in their financial aspirations: some are primarily interested in the practice of their profession and have few financial goals beyond making a good living and accumulating a retirement fund; others aspire to build up a substantial net worth that will give them financial independence. This latter type of client, in particular, will need a close working relationship with the accountant in the analysis of investment opportunities and planning of financial goals.

5. Goals should be put in writing. Stating financial goals in written form will generally yield better results than will oral discussion only. The accountant can provide a format of information to be put in writing; see Exhibit 10-1 for a suggested format. This should be revised freely and followed only to the extent appropriate. The planning should be flexible to provide for changing circumstances due to the type of clients and their financial situation.

GETTING OFF TO A GOOD START FINANCIALLY

The best time to help a client adopt good financial practices and habits is at the outset of his or her career. The handling of withdrawals or salary, the level of personal expenses, and saving money are all matters that must be addressed early. The practices adopted will indicate where the client is headed financially. The accountant should strive to have some input regarding these and similar matters as early as possible.

Getting the Spouse Involved in Financial Matters

The spouse can have a significant impact on the financial success of the professional. It is important to get the spouse involved in questions of setting financial objectives and determining personal and family financial needs. The involvement of the spouse requires the use of skill in human relations on the part of both the accountant and the client. Spouses differ greatly in their interest in financial matters. Some spouses have considerable interest in the financial area and want to be involved in investment decisions; others have little interest.

The approach to involving the spouse must be determined by the circumstances and the nature of the individuals involved; the potential methods vary widely. There are several basic steps, however, that apply to all situations:

1. Determine the interest and aptitude of the spouse in financial matters.
2. Determine the spending habits of the spouse.
3. Determine the areas of family financial requirements for which the spouse will be responsible.
4. Determine the amount of funds available for personal financial use.

A review of these matters, preferably with both the client and spouse, will permit establishment of some basic guidelines. These guidelines should enable the spouse to know the amount of money available and the purposes for which it should be spent. These guidelines should be reached by agreement of both spouses and with an understanding on the part of both that it is a step in achieving financial goals and avoiding financial problems.

If the spouse has financial ability and aptitude, these traits should be utilized in the most suitable manner. Some spouses have the ability to keep tax and financial records. Others can play an important role by taking the time and effort to study investment alternatives, following up on investments already made, etc. Certainly, the financial talents of the spouse should be fully utilized. When both spouses are contributing financially, both should have a voice in setting financial goals. If one spouse has a spending problem, this becomes difficult to control when the spending is financed by his or her own earnings. If there are differences of opinion on spending habits or financial plans they may be more difficult to reconcile than in the situation of a nonworking spouse.

Advising Two Working Spouses

Two working spouses will have more money available. They presumably also have the basic talent and ability to make financial plans, if properly guided.

The accountant's work may be more closely involved with one spouse than the other. He should, therefore, use that relationship as the vehicle for initiating financial planning involving both spouses. He must handle these sessions with skill, determining which spouse has the most aptitude and interest in financial matters, which is the strongest personality, etc.

The family with two working spouses is encountered more and more frequently. This situation presents planning opportunities that are unique and challenging. As stated above, working out a financial plan involving two breadwinners can be more difficult than with one. Dealing with two working spouses must be anticipated by the accountant who engages in this type of practice.

The Choice Between Present and Future Needs

Financial planning and discipline require a trade-off—a balancing of the need to satisfy present-day desires and wants and the need to save and invest for the future. Many of us would like to satisfy our current desires by spending all we make. Some actually spend all, or more, than current income. But most discipline themselves to save. The accountant should be sure the client and spouse understand this point.

Taking Inventory—Determining Current Financial Position

The best way to start the financial planning process is to determine the client's current financial position. This may be a relatively simple procedure, depending on the complexity of the client's financial affairs. For the younger professional, it may not be too difficult. It is basically a matter of preparing a personal financial statement.

Be sure to explain clearly what you are doing and the reason. Explain that in order to see where we are headed we need to know where we stand now. We need to make a list of all significant assets and of all liabilities. This can then be accomplished by working with whatever records are available.

Particular care should be taken to ascertain all liabilities, both actual and contingent. Inquiry should be made into new liabilites that might be incurred in the near term. Detailed listings should be made of the various liabilities. The liability schedule should include obligations to make charitable contributions, to assist family members financially, etc.

Easily Overlooked Assets and Liabilities

Certain types of assets and liabilities can easily be overlooked. Some of these are:

- Cash value of life insurance
- Valuable paintings, coin and stamp collections, antiques
- Vested interest in retirement funds
- Personal loans to and/or from individuals
- Contents of safe deposit box

When preparing this information, it is a good time to prepare a schedule of insurance coverage, if the client does not already have one. An evaluation of the coverage may be appropriate, although an insurance expert should be brought in to review any conclusions.

A schedule of credit cards by the client is also in order at this point. Overuse of credit cards can create financial havoc, and it is important to determine what the client is doing in this area.

As a guide to the client and the accountant, Exhibit 10-2 provides forms that can be used.

Taking Inventory—Determining Spending Habits

A significant part of the process of determining where the client stands financially is a review of present spending habits. It is impossible to plan for future spending without knowing what is being spent currently.

This may be a tedious and time-consuming exercise, since most clients do not keep records on personal spending. The accountant should attempt to get the client or spouse to do the necessary analysis, rather than spending his or her own time on it.

An attempt should be made to prepare a monthly analysis of the client's personal spending over a twelve-month period. This is a prelude to the important step of setting up a personal budget.

Setting Up a Personal Budget

The client who is serious about establishment of sound financial goals and controlling unnecessary personal spending should be willing to establish a personal budget. If the client is unwilling to do this, it is questionable whether a planning program will succeed.

The way in which budgeting is approached and the extent of detail used can vary from client to client. Some clients may do effective budgeting in a general way, preferring not to get into too much detail. If this approach suits the client, it should be followed.

If either the client or spouse is willing and has the inclination to maintain spending records in reasonable detail, an effective control of personal expenditures can be made.

A budget worksheet such as that shown in Exhibit 10-3 should be used, providing for budget figures on a monthly basis, with an adjoining column for entering actual expenditures.

For clients who show reluctance to get involved in this kind of record keeping it can be explained that it is not necessary to continue it year after year. Once a pattern of spending control is set up for a year or two, it is normal to maintain the same pattern, whether an annual budget is used or not. Clients who succeed in establishing spending control, therefore, may very well discontinue the use of a formal budget process after a year or two.

Even if the formal budget process is abandoned, however, it is still important to see where the client stands on an annual basis, as described in the following paragraphs.

Importance of Knowing Where the Client Stands Financially

The most basic tool in keeping up the client's financial progress is the preparation of an annual financial statement. Such a statement determines the progress of assets, liabilities and net worth on an annual basis, permitting a comparison with prior years. Satisfactory financial progress requires an increase in net worth at a rate in excess of the current inflation rate.

Some clients of the writer maintain records of annual financial statements covering a period of many years. Such historical records covering an extended period provide clear evidence of the client's financial progress.

Financial statement preparation should be done on an annual basis—not spasmodically. Only on an annual basis can comparisons be made, giving the desired picture of the client's progress.

A columnar presentation providing for a comparison over a period of five or more years should be used for the most effective comparison.

GUIDING THE CLIENT IN THE USE OF CREDIT

Virtually all professional clients use credit at some time during their careers. It is important for them to know how and when to use credit, and to be aware of the dangers of too much credit.

The use of credit in the professional practice itself was discussed in Chapter 3. The following discussion covers use of credit for investment and personal purposes.

Use of Credit for Personal Purposes

Clients do not normally consult their accountants regarding personal purchases and the financing of them. Any discussion of this kind would probably come up in connection with financial planning, budget preparation, and the like. The accountant, however, may choose to bring up the subject himself when he sees the client overextending himself.

It may be desirable to discuss the following points on the subject of personal credit:

- Purposes for which personal credit should be incurred, including what kind of purchases should be made with credit and which ones should be postponed until cash can be paid
- Amount of credit that can be handled without creating problems
- Cost of credit

- Control of use of credit cards and revolving charge accounts
- The role played by the spouse in the use of credit

The central theme of a discussion of this subject should be the control of use of credit for purchases of luxuries or unnecessary items. The accountant can point out the financial cost and strains brought on by excessive credit, as well as the need to postpone certain purchases until capital has been accumulated for other purposes.

Use of Credit for Investments

For the client who is investment oriented and interested in building up a substantial estate, the use of credit is a necessity. Building up a portfolio of investments without the use of credit is very difficult.

The client should be made aware that while the use of credit is essential, it has its pitfalls. The pitfalls relate to the quality of investment itself, because a poor investment can create a financial setback. The availability of credit, morever, may provide a temptation to invest. The client with credit readily available must not be lulled into a false sense of security and must be judicious in selecting his or her investments.

The accountant will be likely to assist the client in reviewing proposed investments, and the use of credit for this purpose should be part of the review. Some points to be covered:

- Review the proposed cash flow from the investment, whether it will be sufficient to retire the debt.

- Review the possibility that the investment might not be able to generate the anticipated cash flow, and what the client would do if this proves to be the case.

- If the client must repay the debt from his own resources, rather than from cash flow from the investment, review his ability to do so.

- Review any tax saving arising from the investment and the extent to which this saving will provide funds to retire the debt.

- Review the cost of credit as compared with the proposed return on the investment, making sure the cost of credit will not offset the return itself.

Setting Limits on Debt

The accountant should help the client determine the limits beyond which he will not go in incurring debt. These limits should be determined according to the client's resources and philosophy concerning risk taking. The approach will vary in each case, but here is an example:

- Mortgage payments on the personal residence should not exceed 25% of annual income.

- Payments on debt incurred for personal purchases (automobiles, appliances, furniture, etc.) should not exceed 10% of annual income.

- Debt repayment on financing of investments should not exceed 20% of annual income.

Such percentages are obviously subject to much variation among clients. The point being made here is not the percentage itself, but the approach to setting limits on debt. The client will be better off if he has certain guidelines to follow.

GUIDING THE CLIENT ON INVESTMENT DECISIONS

Where to get investment advice—The accountant with a professional client interested in investments will probably become involved in advising the client on investment decisions. The accountant should not attempt to be the sole investment adviser by any means, and should suggest the use of other advisers. Advice on investment decisions can come from a number of sources, from which the accountant can recommend the most suitable:

- Real estate agents
- Stock brokers and investment firms
- Bankers and lawyers
- Other clients and associates in the business community who have investments or are knowledgeable about opportunities.

As stated at the outset of this chapter, some advisers derive commission income from the investment decision. While their advice may be sound, it should be reviewed by someone who is working solely for the client.

Helping the Client Evaluate Investment Opportunities

The investment opportunities available to clients cover a wide range. The evaluation of them, therefore, must depend on the circumstances and the type of investment offered. No hard and fast rules can be laid down, but some general principles can be applied to various situations.

The first order of business should be to caution the client to approach any investment as serious business, requiring thorough and deliberate consideration. Impulsive and hasty actions should be avoided. Investments should be studied carefully and systemically.

The matter of making investments for tax benefits can be dangerous. The client can become enthusiastic about the tax savings and fail to properly investigate the quality of the investment itself. The quality of the investment should be considered first, with the potential tax benefit a secondary consideration.

The client should be advised that a good investment may provide a temporary tax shelter, but that eventually it will create taxable income. A poor investment on the other hand, yields tax savings but leaves the investor less well off financially.

In reviewing any investment, the following factors should be considered. While the order of importance of these factors varies with different investments and investors, the order in which they are listed can be used as a guide to their relative importance.

Location. Investments far from home should be approached cautiously. It is more difficult to visit the investment and evaluate its progress. There are exceptions, of course, and investments in growing, prosperous localities are to be encouraged in the right circumstances. For some types of investments, such as real estate, location is of prime importance. In other cases, such factors as the economics of a particular industry should receive prime consideration.

Asking price. The price to be paid is most important. It is difficult to make a successful investment when paying a premium price going in. This requires careful evaluation and the exercise of judgment. The investor does not want to overpay, but, on the other hand, must be aware that good investment opportunities are lost by being too conservative regarding price.

Cash commitment. The client must determine whether he is able to meet the cash commitment. Some investments require not only an initial cash payment, but a commitment for future payments. The entire commitment must be considered.

Debt commitment. The subject of going into debt to finance investments has been discussed earlier. The debt commitment is an important consideration that must be thoroughly explored.

Potential return and risk. Return and risk generally go hand in hand; the greater the potential return the greater the risk. The client's financial resources and personal inclinations toward risk taking are the factors to be considered in reviewing this area. The accountant should strive to keep the client wary of investments with sufficient risk and financial commitment to create financial problems.

Liquidity. The liquidity of an investment can either add to or detract from its attractiveness. Here again, the client's age and financial outlook are factors to consider in deciding on the extent to go into investments with limited liquidity.

Tax effect. The tax effect of the investment should be analyzed. This subject has been discussed in Chapter 6. The tax outlook is where the accountant is most likely to be brought into the picture. When the subject of the tax effect is brought up, it provides an opportunity to explore the other aspects of the investment with the client.

Investing in Limited Partnerships. In recent years a popular investment vehicle has been the limited partnership. Limited partnerships usually provide tax benefits in the early years, limit the liability of the investor, are easy to get into, frequently can be sold if a need arises, and relieve the investor of management responsibilities.

Limited partnerships offer investment opportunities in numerous lines—real estate, oil drilling, equipment leasing, cattle, magazine publishing, and many others. They are generally marketed through stock brokerage houses with heavy emphasis on the tax benefits.

The accountant advising his client should investigate these areas:

1. Reputation and Track Record of the General Partner. The general partner usually is the organizer and promoter of the project. He should be experienced in the field in which the partnership will operate. He should have a record of performance in previous projects of the same type.

2. Financial Arrangements Between the General Partner and Limited Partners. Some limited partnerships are structured so that the general partner's share of profits is so large it is difficult for the limited partners to earn a good return. Investigation should be made into the division of profits between the general partner and the limited partners, as well as the compensation to be paid the general partner.

It is also wise to investigate the amount of capital being put up by the general partner. A project in which the general partner is not risking capital along with the limited partners should be looked at carefully.

Potential Liability as a Partner. Some limited partnership agreements state that limited partners can be assessed additional capital contributions under certain circumstances. This point should be looked into so that the client knows what his potential liability could be.

How to Get Out and When. The partnership agreement should be studied as to provisions for selling a partnership interest. If the client is to be locked in for a number of years this should be clearly understood, as should provisions whereby the interest can be sold if necessary.

Importance of Investment Opportunities

Investments are important to professional clients. Most professional practices do not require large amounts of capital and the practitioner usually has funds to invest. The experienced professional man with a good income, particularly, is in the market for investment opportunities. Frequently, exposure of these clients to investment opportunities is limited and they are looking to various sources for ideas.

The accountant can not only make suggestions regarding investment opportunities, but, more important, can help the client in evaluating such opportunities.

PREPARATION FOR INTERRUPTION OF INCOME

A serious potential problem faced by professional clients is interruption of income due to illness or accident. Loss of income can create financial havoc. The client's financial planning should by all means cover this potential hazard.

Emergency Cash Fund

It was stated earlier in this chapter that one of the client's financial objectives should be to have an emergency fund on hand to cover expenses for three to six months. The question of whether this fund should be sufficient to cover only personal expenses, or both personal expenses and office overhead, should be discussed.

Income Protection Through Group Practice

As stated in Chapter 9, one of the advantages of group practice is the likelihood of an income protection clause in the group's agreement. The members of the group usually agree to continue to pay the income of a disabled member for a specified period of time. Planning for the possibility of loss of income should, therefore, include a review of any benefits available from this source.

Insurance Covering Loss of Income

Professional clients should consider the need for insurance covering loss of income due to disability. Such coverage is a real financial life saver when the need for it arises. The client should be advised of the importance of this type of insurance coverage. The following points should be considered in connection with it:

Income protection policies are available with a variety of waiting periods before benefits are paid. A longer waiting period results in a considerable saving in premium. A review should be made of the waiting period that will best suit the client's financial situation.

The definition of disability as described in the policy should be reviewed. It is important to understand how the policy defines disability, so the insured will know what to expect in case of ability to work part time or some other variable.

Some disability policies are designed to be tax deductible and some are not. If the premium is deductible, the proceeds are generally taxable, and vice versa. Policies with deductible premiums are generally designed to pay office overhead expenses.

PLANNING FOR RETIREMENT

All financial planning leads to the goal of achieving financial independence, which in turn leads to the option of retirement whenever desired. This entire chapter, therefore, can be considered to be dealing with retirement planning. A complete discussion of personal financial planning, however, requires a specific discussion of certain points regarding retirement.

Determining Financial Needs

The fact that the client has a retirement plan for tax-saving purposes shouldn't preclude additional financial planning for retirement. It is possible that the retirement plan won't provide sufficient retirement income. The possibility of being required to shoulder financial responsibility for others, such as parents, even in retirement years should be considered. In short, the financial picture for retirement needs should be reviewed well in advance of the retirement date to determine resources available and the level of income needed.

The involvement of the accountant will require the client to think about these problems and plan more carefully. The accountant can guide the client in the thinking and planning process and help him reach decisions and conclusions he might otherwise overlook.

Tax Planning. An important area of retirement planning is anticipation of income tax liability. The withdrawal of funds from a retirement plan in particular needs careful tax planning. The client generally has the choice of taking his retirement benefits in one of several ways:

• Rolling the funds over into an Individual Retirement Account with the view of leaving them to accumulate tax free for a few more years (this has both advantages and disadvantages)

- Taking a lump sum distribution and computing the tax on one of the "averaging" provisions of the tax law
- Taking the benefits in monthly installments

The ongoing income tax picture should also be considered. The retired client doesn't want the tax collector to take a major bite out of his retirement funds. The potential level of taxable income and tax brackets should be reviewed. If the tax burdens warrant it, consideration should be given to getting into tax-free income, tax shelters, or diverting income to others. While retired persons are not generally interested in tax shelters or diverting income to others, these possibilities should not be ruled out.

Preparing a Written Plan

Once these matters have been discussed with the client, a report should be prepared in writing. Stating the plan in writing makes it more meaningful for the client. Such a written report is found in Exhibit 10-4.

FINANCIAL GOALS

Financially, my goals are to: Resources required

a. Purchase a first class residence $_____

b. Provide a nest egg for emergencies $_____

c. Provide funds for education of children $_____

d. Accumulate funds for investment $_____

e. Become financially independent $_____

f. Provide funds for retirement at age ____ $_____

g. Provide for family security in event of untimely death $_____

PROFESSIONAL GOALS
(Where do I want to be in my profession, and what steps must I take to achieve these goals)

Next year:_____

In five years:_____

_____

In ten years:_____

_____

Personal goals (in such areas as family activities, civic activities, hobbies, leisure time, etc.)

Next year:_____

_____

In five years:_____

_____

In ten years:_____

_____

Exhibit 10-1: Goal-Setting Worksheet

ASSETS

CASH OR EQUIVALENT	Current Year	Prior Year	Increase (Decrease)
Savings accounts	$	$	$
Personal checking accounts			
Life insurance cash value			

SECURITIES

Stocks (common and preferred)			
Mutual funds			
Bonds			
Other			

REAL ESTATE

Home			
Vacation home			
Investment properties			

OTHER INVESTMENTS

Professional practice			
Retirement trust			
Business investments			
Tax shelter investments			

OTHER PROPERTY

Home furnishings			
Cars			
Boats, planes, recreational equipment			
Jewelry, furs			
Collections (art, coins, stamps, books, etc.)			

DEBTS OWED TO YOU			
ANY OTHER ASSETS			
Total assets	$	$	$

Exhibit 10-2: Personal Financial Statement

LIABILITIES

MORTGAGES OUTSTANDING	Current Year	Prior Year	Increase (Decrease)
Home	$	$	$
Vacation home			
Investment properties			

LOANS OUTSTANDING (See schedule)

Bank

Broker

Insurance policy loans

Other

TAXES

Federal

State

County

City

Other

BILLS OUTSTANDING

ANY OTHER DEBTS

Total liabilities	$	$	$
Net worth (assets minus liabilities)	$	$	$
Percentage of increase or decrease ("Change" divided by prior net worth) %			%

Outstanding Loans

	Name	Date	Principal Amount	Int %	No. of Pmts.	Date Due	Comments
1.							
2.							
3.							
4.							
5.							
6.							

Exhibit 10-2: Personal Financial Statement (Continued)

Charitable Contributions and Contingent Liabilities

	Name	Amount	Due Date	Comments
1.				
2.				
3.				
4.				
5.				
6.				

General Insurance Information
Auto, Homeowners, Jewelry, Liability, etc.

	Coverage	Amount or Limits	Term in years	Expires	Company	Policy number	Premium	Comment
1.								
2.								
3.								
4.								
5.								
6.								
7.								
8.								
9.								
10.								
11.								

Medical, Surgical, Major Medical Insurance

	Hosp. room & board	Surgical schedule	Major med. max.	Deductible co.-ins.	Company	Policy number	Premium	Comments- Expires
1.								
2.								
3.								
4.								

Exhibit 10-2: Personal Financial Statement (Continued)

Credit Cards, Charge Cards Record   **(If lost or stolen)**

	Company	Number	Fee	% Int.	Expires	If missing, notify:
1.						
2.						
3.						
4.						
5.						
6.						
7.						
8.						
9.						
10.						
11.						
12.						
13.						
14.						
15.						

Exhibit 10-2: Personal Financial Statement (Continued)

	JANUARY BUDGET ACTUAL	FEBRUARY BUDGET ACTUAL
INCOME		
1 Salary or withdrawal from practice		
2 Bonus		
3 Miscellaneous		
4 Interest		
5 Dividends		
6 Rents		
7 Short-Term Gains		
8 Long-Term Gains		
9 Pension/Profit Sharing		
10 Disability/Insurance		
11 TOTAL INCOME		
EXPENSES		
12 Business Expense		
13 Accounting/Legal		
14 Interest		
15 Charitable Contributions		
16 Medical & Dental		
17 Property Taxes		
18 Federal Income Tax		
19 State Income Tax		
20 Social Security Insurance		
21 General Casualty Insurance		
22 Life Insurance		
23 Rents		
24 Children's Education		
25 Family Assistance/Alimony		
26 Household Expenses		
27 Recreation, Trips, Clubs		
28 TOTAL EXPENSES		
29 EXCESS OF INCOME OVER EXPENSES		
INVESTMENTS		
30 Savings Account		
31 Business Interests		
32 Home Improvement		
33 Auto		
34 Recreation Equipment		
35 Stocks, Bonds, Mutual Funds		
36 Tax Shelters		
37		
38 TOTAL INVESTED		

Exhibit 10-3: Budget Worksheet

Dr. Louis Kent
Brownsville, Texas

Dear Dr. Kent:

After our recent review and analysis of your financial objectives I think the highlights of our discussions and conclusions should be put in writing. This will serve as a reminder to both of us regarding your goals and objectives and will help stimulate additional thought.

Your objectives, based on present levels of income and family status, were determined to be:

1. Maintain your present standard of living.
2. Provide for the college education of your children, which will be completed in approximately 10, 12, and 13 years.
3. Provide funds to permit foreign and domestic travel beginning within a year or two.
4. Build up adequate resources to cover an emergency, illness, or untimely death.
5. Provide a retirement fund which will permit a reduced workload or complete retirement, if desired, in about fifteen years.

Your current needs on a monthly basis were determined to be as follows:

house payments	$ 600.00
food	500.00
clothing	300.00
insurance	500.00
transportation	300.00
school	200.00
recreation	200.00
other	500.00
	$ 3,100.00

In addition to the above requirements you must pay your income tax and provide for the objectives outlined above.

Income tax and self-employment tax on your current income of $90,000 is expected to run about $34,000 per year. Your financial situation, therefore, is something like this:

Exhibit 10-4: Letter to Client Regarding Financial Plan

Current income		$90,000
Living expense	$37,200	
Taxes	34,000	71,200
Remaining Funds		$18,800

The balance of $18,800 would appear at first glance to be adequate for providing for the other objectives. Upon closer examination, however, it will take considerable effort on your part to meet all your goals. They are within reach only if you plan well and start putting your plan into effect now.

A substantial drain on your income now and in future years is the tax burden. There are certain steps that can be taken to ease this burden, and that should be started immediately.

Setting up a retirement plan. I recommend that you set up a Keogh type retirement plan and start contributing $7,500 per year. Not only are the contributions tax deductible, the earnings compound tax free until withdrawn. A contribution of $7,500 per year, with earnings compounding at 10%, will provide a retirement fund of some $200,000 after fifteen years. In your present tax bracket the annual contribution will take only $3,750 from your spendable income, the other $3,750 representing tax saving.

Setting up a ten-year trust for your children. I recommend that you transfer your office building to a ten-year trust for the benefit of your children. You will then rent the building from the trust at a reasonable rental, which will yield an annual income of $6,000 to the trust. This will, in effect, divert $6,000 of taxable income annually to your children for the next ten years to be used by your children for their college education. This totals $54,750, plus accumulated interest. While this amount is not sufficient to cover the full cost, it will go a long way.

After implementing these two programs, your financial situation will look something like this:

Current income		$90,000
Less: retirement contribution	$7,500	
rent on office building	6,000	13,500
Adjusted income		76,500
Living expense	37,200	
Taxes	27,250	64,450
Remaining Funds		$12,050

You will have put away $6,000 for children's education and $7,500 for retirement and still have $12,050 available for investment or saving. You have also reduced your tax burden by $6,750 per year.

These two steps will assist greatly in meeting your financial objectives. The excess funds can be used to make investments or build up your cash reserves. They could also be used as a vehicle for making tax shelter investments if you are so inclined, which we can discuss further when you are ready.

One further point: I feel your present income and expense picture provides a good relationship between funds available for current living expenses, retirement needs, and children's education. As the years go by, your income will probably continue to increase. I

Exhibit 10-4: Letter to Client Regarding Financial Plan (Continued)

recommend that you maintain this relationship, providing for increases not only in your standard of living but also in investment funds.

In regard to your objective of having adequate resources in case of serious illness or untimely death, I recommend that you look into a $150,000 fifteen-year reducing term life insurance policy. This will cost considerably less than whole life coverage, and will provide reducing amounts of insurance on an annual basis as you build your resources and as your children approach college graduation. In other words, the insurance coverage goes down as your other resources build up and your responsibilities decrease.

Working with you on this plan has been an enjoyable and satisfying experience. I suggest we look at it again in about two years to see how you are doing and if changes are needed.

Exhibit 10-4: Letter to Client Regarding Financial Plan (Continued)

11

Planning the Estate
of the Professional

The term "estate planning" covers many areas of the client's financial affairs. The term itself may be an unfortunate choice of words, since it implies planning for death. Estate planning covers much more than that, a point which should be made to the client as early as possible.

Estate planning is a specialized field that requires training and expertise. An accountant with limited skills in the field can easily get in over his head. Before undertaking estate planning engagements the accountant should participate in professional seminars and get experience by working with an experienced practitioner.

Estate planning for the professional client in many respects is similar to that for the nonprofessional. There are certain distinctions, however, that should be borne in mind. The professional has a valuable asset in the form of his professional license and his ability to practice his profession. This asset has some significant restrictions on it, however. It cannot be transferred and it is of value only during the active professional life of the practitioner. A professional practice, therefore, cannot utilize certain estate planning techniques normally used by the owners of commercial businesses. These distinctions are pointed out in the discussions that follow.

GETTING STARTED

The accountant is frequently the first person to observe a potential estate problem. His knowledge of the client's financial affairs makes it natural to develop an awareness of estate tax problems such as the likelihood of a large estate tax liability or a lack of liquidity. Indeed, part of the accountant's experience in this field leads to development of an awareness of estate problems when reviewing a client's financial statements or tax returns.

One method of staying abreast of this and other areas in which the client needs tax planning services is using a checklist for additional services the client might require.

Our firm requires that such a checklist be reviewed in connection with preparation of client income tax returns, and has found it quite useful in identifying additional services that are needed. See Exhibit 11-1 for this checklist.

The practical time to discuss estate planning is when it will flow naturally into the conversation. There are a number of such times that can be utilized by the alert accountant:

- When the client asks about gift taxes.
- When client brings up the subject of estate taxes or estate planning.
- When discussing a purchase or sale of the professional practice.
- During income tax discussions, either tax planning sessions or the income tax return interview.
- During preparation of the personal financial statement.
- When discussing bringing in a partner, going into group practice, or related matters.

How to Approach the Client About Estate Planning

The matter of estate planning can be brought up on any number of occasions, as stated in the preceding paragraphs. Pick a time when the figures are clearly in the client's mind and he will be receptive to consideration of estate planning.

The client's age and financial status are important. Clients over age fifty generally are more receptive to estate planning. A person with a substantial net worth, however, should be concerned with estate planning at any age.

The accountant must anticipate resistance on the part of some clients. Some of the reasons for resistance:

- Dislike of a subject that relates to planning for death.
- Unwillingness to take the time.
- A misconception of what estate planning is all about.
- A feeling that this is something that can be put off.
- A feeling that everything is in order because of having a will, life insurance coverage, etc.
- Resistance to incurring the expense.

Resistance can be overcome by pointing out the advantages and objectives to be accomplished, as discussed below.

Objectives of Estate Planning
That Your Client Should Know About

The accountant should explain clearly and positively the objectives of estate planning. The point can be made that estate planning has significant lifetime benefits for the client himself, as well as important benefits for his family after he is gone. Some of the benefits:

1. Planning increases the chances that one's estate will be distributed in the manner desired; to the right people, at the right time, in the right manner.

2. Planning minimizes the possibility of complications and disputes following the client's death.

3. Planning makes it possible to anticipate the tax burden and take steps to minimize it.

4. Planning helps determine the need for liquidity in time to do something about it.

5. Planning provides for better management of resources, which usually results in lifetime benefits through more retirement income.

6. Planning gives more peace of mind because of the good feeling of knowing one's affairs are in order.

Persuading the Client to Incur the Cost

A question the client will logically ask is about the cost of estate planning service. The accountant should base his answer on the value of the service, rather than trying to minimize the dollar cost. It is a virtual certainty that estate planning will save the client considerable money, which point should be emphasized.

Estate work is a specialized field requiring training and experience. The accountant normally charges a premium fee for this kind of work. Further, he must perform the job thoroughly, taking sufficient time to gather all facts and analyze alternative solutions. Trying to keep the fee down can result in shortchanging certain steps. The end result can be a less than thorough job, which will do the accountant and the client an injustice.

The accountant's approach to the fee question, therefore, should be positive. Point out the benefits and savings; at the same time, discuss frankly the rates to be charged and the potential amount of time the job may require. It is always best to give the client an estimate as to the amount of fee expected, rather than to surprise him at the end of the job.

Psychology in Estate Planning

Throughout this book, mention has been made of the need on the part of the accountant to develop human relations skills in dealing with various clients of diverse personalities and backgrounds. Estate planning is clearly an area where such skills are of utmost importance—perhaps more so than elsewhere. Several points can be made in regard to utilizing those skills in estate planning work:

Always respect the client's wishes. A person has the right to use and leave his property as he sees fit. Some clients feel that estate taxes coming due after they die should be dealt with by the heirs. They don't want to rearrange their affairs to save taxes that someone else will pay. If the client feels strongly about this, the accountant should respect his wishes.

Develop an ability to understand the other person's feelings. A discussion of estate planning involves the disposition of the client's property and the consideration of death. People react to this in different ways. The effective adviser must be attuned to the client's reactions.

The estate adviser should be a genuinely caring person with a sincere interest in the client's problem. This is the best way to do an effective job and come out with a feeling of satisfaction.

GOING ABOUT THE JOB

After the subject has been initially discussed with the client, and he realizes he has a need for estate planning services, it is time to get on with the job. The management of the engagement is important to its success, and certain steps and techniques should be observed.

Choosing Advisers to Work With

The accountant, of course, cannot do the complete job himself. An attorney will be involved in the entire process, participating in discussions and drafting legal instruments. Life insurance agents and trust officers may come into the picture as needed.

The accountant is the adviser who generally has the closest relationship with the client. He is in regular contact regarding income tax and financial matters. He is most likely to spot the need for estate planning and to initiate the discussions. He has the best picture of the client's finances and potential estate problems. He frequently is, therefore, the key adviser.

The estate planning process needs one person who coordinates the various activities (assuming a number of advisers are involved) and keeps things moving. The accountant is frequently the logical person because of deep involvement in the matter and his key position as described above.

If the client requests the accountant to recommend advisers certain criteria should be kept in mind. An attorney should be recommended who is oriented toward business and/or tax work, as opposed to extensive trial work. He should be experienced and knowledgeable in wills, and in trust and estate matters. A life insurance agent should be chosen who takes a professional approach to his work, who is objective, and who considers the client's well-being of as much importance as the selling of insurance.

Need for Full Disclosure

At the outset of estate planning the client should be told in a tactful manner that full disclosure is essential. There is a reluctance on the part of some clients to disclose certain information; in other cases the client may overlook certain data. It is imperative that the advisers have all the facts.

The accountant will have to be guided in this matter by his relationship with the client. In some instances it may be unnecessary to bring it up at all. In other instances it should be mentioned only to motivate the client not to overlook needed information. Only in rare instances would a valued, reputable client deliberately withhold information.

Inventorying the Potential Assets of the Estate

The first step in gathering facts is to inventory the potential assets of the estate. This is similar, but not identical, to the preparation of a personal financial statement. If the client has been preparing an annual personal financial statement as discussed in Chapter 10 the inventorying process will be greatly enhanced.

The personal financial statement can serve as a starting point, but additional information must be obtained. Some of the items are:

- Amount of life insurance proceeds that will be includible in the estate.
- Consideration of articles of value that might not be included on the financial statement, such as collections of stamps or coins, works of art, valuable antiques, jewelry, silver, gold, etc.
- Articles of value kept in a safe deposit box that might be overlooked unless specifically mentioned or sought out.

A questionnaire, such as the one found in Exhibit 11-2, is helpful in gathering data.

Preparing a Financial Projection for the Estate

Such a projection uses as a starting point the information developed from the inventory described above. Once the total potential assets and liabilities of the estate are determined, a projection must be made of the potential estate tax liability.

A review must be made of which assets will be taxed and which will not. In community property states, consideration should be given to separate and community property of the spouses. The utilization of the marital deduction must be considered, as should ownership and taxability of life insurance proceeds.

A comprehensive discussion of the principles of estate taxation is beyond the scope of this book, but suffice it to say that an accountant undertaking this type of engagement must be knowledgeable in the subject. To do so without the necessary training and experience is a disservice to the client.

The final result of the financial projection reflects the amounts available after taxes for distributions to beneficiaries, trusts, contributions, or whatever the client has in mind. Inventorying the estate and preparing the projection leads to consideration of estate planning techniques to be used to achieve the client's objectives and to reduce the estate tax burden.

PRINCIPLES TO FOLLOW IN ESTATE PLANNING

Most estate planning ideas are for the purpose of saving taxes. Such ideas are many and varied, some valid and some of dubious quality. Tax saving ideas will continue to proliferate as long as tax rates are high enough to make it profitable for imaginative estate planners to develop them. The accountant must stay abreast of this field but must be wary of those ideas that are unproven and may bring on problems. The techniques described below are of proven validity and have worked for others.

In suggesting estate tax saving ideas to the client, the accountant is well advised to keep these principles in mind:

Keep It Simple. Some practitioners yield to the temptation to develop an involved estate plan utilizing various sophisticated technqiues. While this is desirable and necessary in some cases, it is usually best to keep the plan as simple as possible. It is possible to devise a plan so complicated that the client can't understand it. This can do more harm than good by creating confusion and potential hard feelings among the beneficiaries.

Be Sure the Client Retains the Resources He Needs. It is tempting to suggest that the client divest himself of certain assets through gifts, trusts, etc. Some persons have done so to the extent that they later regretted it. Everyone should be advised to retain sufficient assets to live out his life comfortably, without concern about having to rely on others for help in case of emergency. A client who divests himself of more than this is making a mistake.

SOME ESTATE PLANNING TECHNIQUES

Use of Annual Gifts. Gifts provide a simple and effective approach to reducing the estate. Annual gifts within the annual exclusion to each of several family members can amount to a substantial sum over a period of years. The client should be advised to give property with a potential for appreciation, if possible, so the appreciation will accrue to the donee. Gifts in excess of the annual exclusion should also be considered in the form of property that is appreciating in value. Professional clients are generally prohibited from making gifts of an interest in their practice, so should look to investment property as a source. A gift of income-producing property not only reduces the estate but reduces current taxable income. A program of gifts, therefore, is a high priority estate planning tool for most clients.

Buy/Sell Agreements. Professional clients engaged in group practice normally have a buy/sell agreement (see further discussion in Chapter 9). The agreement establishes the price to be paid to the estate of a deceased practitioner for his share of the practice, thus establishing the value of the practice for estate tax purposes. The accountant should recommend the use of a buy/sell agreement to the professional client.

Retirement Plan Benefits. Retirement plan benefits can be excluded from the taxable estate if not paid as a lump sum and if paid to a beneficiary other than the estate. Any estate planning program should consider this, although the decision as to type of payment can be made after death.

Asset Value Freeze. The asset value freeze technique generally involves creating additional classes of stock for the family business, transferring stock that appreciates in value to children. The stock retained by the parents has characteristics which hold its value unchanged. The company's growth is attributed to younger family members. Such an arrangement is difficult to work for a professional practice. If the client has developed other business interests or investments, however, this device may have potential.

Private Annuities. The private annuity is a complex, but effective, method of reducing a taxable estate. It is not often used when disposing of a professional practice, but could be used if the parties agree. It is particularly effective for selling a farm or closely held business to family members. The private annuity, stated in its simplest terms, is a transer of property where the buyer promises to make payments throughout the seller's life. The buyer pays a monthly or annual payment to the seller until the seller dies. The sale must be at fair market value and the annuity payments based on the seller's life expectancy. A private annuity has certain income tax implications for both the buyer and seller that must be considered. It is obvious, however, that an obligation that ceases upon the seller's death removes the asset from his estate. The practitioner involved in estate planning must be familiar with private annuities and be prepared to offer this alternative.

Flower Bonds. Flower bonds are certain designated U.S. Government bonds available on the market, generally at a discount, which can be surrendered at par in payment of estate tax liability. They must be owned at date of death to be used in this manner. The taxpayer can buy bonds prior to death at a discount and his executor can use them at par to pay estate tax. They must be included in his estate tax return at par. This is an effective planning device in the right circumstances.

USE OF TRUSTS

The trust is a flexible tool with many varied uses. It is particularly suitable in connection with financial planning and estate planning.

A trust can be used to provide resources and income to a family member who is sick or disabled, or who lacks investment and management skills. A husband can leave the estate to his wife in trust if he feels she lacks the skill to manage the assets or needs protection from those who might take advantage of her.

A trust can provide for distributions of property after the death of the grantor if he feels property should not be distributed on his death. A trust can by law (in most states) last throughout the lifetime of the beneficiary plus twenty-one years.

A trust can be used to transfer property during lifetime in order to avoid probate.

Some specific types of trusts the accountant should consider in estate planning for the professional client are briefly described below:

Testamentary Bypass Trust. A spouse by will leaves property in trust to the other spouse rather than leaving it outright. This keeps the estate from doubling up on the death of the second spouse. The surviving spouse receives income from the trust for life, with the principal passing to the children upon death.

Life Insurance Trust. Owns life insurance policies and receives the proceeds upon death, thus keeping these funds out of the taxable estate. The trust uses the proceeds to loan funds to or buy assets from the estate, or passes them along to beneficiaries.

Charitable Remainder Trust. Provides both income tax and estate tax benefits. The client places an income-producing asset in trust, with the income to the client for life and the principal to a charitable organization upon death. The asset is removed from the client's estate, and the client gets a current income tax deduction for a charitable contribution (limited to the present value of the future interest).

Living Trusts. A living trust is set up to receive assets from the client during his lifetime. If the trust is irrevocable the assets are removed from the estate as well as providing current income tax savings by diverting the income to others.

The client must relinquish both control of and enjoyment of the assets to effectively remove them from his estate.

For the client who isn't sure of the extent to which he is willing to relinquish enjoyment and control, a revocable living trust could be considered. The client could revoke the trust if he wasn't satisfied with the arrangement. There are no income tax or estate tax savings, but the assets would avoid probate.

When discussing trusts with the client it is always necessary to point out that taxable gifts may result from transferring property to a trust. Further, a trust is a taxable entity and is required to file an income tax return and pay income tax.

There are many opportunities for effective use of trusts and the accountant should develop his expertise in this field to effectively serve his clients. This discussion covers only a few highlights, and additional study of the subject is recommended.

ESTATE PLANNING FOR DEATH OF THE SPOUSE

Most estate planning contemplates the death of the breadwinner and provides for financial security for the surviving spouse and children. Considerably less planning is done in the event that the first death is that of a non-income-producing spouse (usually a wife and mother). There seems to be a feeling that if the husband survives he is still producing income and can, therefore, take care of whatever financial problems develop. While this position has merit, the death of a wife can bring significant financial burdens that should be considered. Some of these are:

- Estate tax liability
- Increased income tax of a nonmarried taxpayer
- Cost of employing someone to assume duties of caring for the household and children
- Cost of last illness and funeral

After the financial effect of these and other costs are evaluated, consideration should be given to any additional planning steps that can be taken. An obvious point to be considered is whether to provide life insurance coverage on the wife and, if so, the amount of such coverage.

ASSISTING WITH LIFE INSURANCE DECISIONS

Life insurance is an area where the client can use help from an adviser other than the life insurance agent. Life insurance coverage comes in many forms, designed to accomplish various purposes. It is sometimes difficult for the client to evaluate the pros and cons of various proposals. The accountant can assist provided he has the knowledge to do so properly.

Determining the Need for Life Insurance Coverage

It is to be anticipated that a life insurance agent who gets involved in estate planning for a client will find a problem that can best be cured by additional life insurance coverage.

If the accountant is asked for advice he must be able to evaluate the proposals, both as to the amount and the type of coverage. Life insurance premiums for clients who have reached the estate planning age are generally expensive. Some techniques discussed elsewhere in this chapter may reduce or eliminate the need for heavy life insurance coverage.

One point to be considered is the period of time during which life insurance coverage is needed. While the client may have a current need for coverage he may expect to become more liquid within five or ten years. In this case term insurance may serve the need. Reducing term can be particularly effective in providing protection during a five- or ten-year period in which liquidity is expected to increase. The professional client can frequently buy group term through his professional association.

While term insurance is attractive, whole life insurance should be considered. Term insurance becomes progressively more expensive as the client gets older, and a client with a projected need for life insurance for many years should consider whole life. Whole life can be financed, if necessary, by borrowing against the policy to pay the premiums.

The need for life insurance is determined in part by the client's age and family status. Life insurance not only provides liquidity for estate tax purposes, it provides income if the breadwinner dies unexpectedly. The younger client most likely will need this type of protection, and whole life may be more suitable because of the long-term nature of his insurance needs.

Keeping Life Insurance Proceeds Out of the Estate

The client who has $100,000 of life insurance coverage would like to think his beneficiaries will get the benefit of $100,000. This won't be the case, however, if the proceeds are taxable in his estate.

There are a number of techniques that can be used to keep life insurance proceeds out of the taxable estate. Two popular methods are:

Place the ownership and control of the policy in the hands of the spouse. For this to be effective, the spouse should pay premimums from her own funds. It may be necessary to make a gift to the spouse to provide these funds. Care must be taken in setting up the procedure for paying premiums to avoid problems with IRS. Also, the spouse must have full ownership and control of the policy.

Have the policy owned by a life insurance trust. This is more involved than ownership by the spouse, but has more flexibility. The trust can use the proceeds to buy assets from or make loans to the estate, or distributions to beneficiaries. It is necessary to set up a trust, name a trustee and determine how the trust will be funded. There are a number of pros and cons to this technique which must be reviewed.

ASSISTING THE CLIENT REGARDING HIS WILL

Although the client's will is a legal matter, the accountant may be in a position to assist. The extent of this assistance will depend on the relationship with the client. If the accountant is closer to the client than the lawyer his input will be helpful and necessary.

Making the Client Will-Conscious

One service the accountant can provide is to make the client conscious of having a will and of keeping it up-to-date. As stated earlier, the entire matter of estate planning is one some clients wish would go away, and this particularly applies to consideration of their wills. Most people figure death is far away, ignoring the possibility of dying unexpectedly. The unexpected death is the situation where unprepared clients leave their families with serious problems.

The accountant is in touch with clients on a more regular basis than the lawyer, and should assume responsibility for reminding clients of the need for an up-to-date will. If the accounting firm has a client bulletin, it can be used effectively for this purpose. Some accounting firms have used a "will quiz" in their client bulletins, like the one found in Exhibit 11-3.

Providing Input into Provisions of the Will

The accountant can use his knowledge of the client's financial status to provide input and ideas concerning the will. He probably knows more about the client's assets than the lawyer, and perhaps in some respects more than the client himself. This, plus his general knowledge of estate planning, makes the accountant's input valuable when provisions of the will are discussed.

The relationship of the accountant and the lawyer, and the respective expertise of each, will affect the nature of input provided by the accountant. Some of the areas where the accountant may provide input are:

- Estate tax-saving techniques
- Naming of an executor or a trustee
- Amount of responsibility to put on the spouse or other family members
- Instructions for disposing of the professional practice, if not covered through a buy and sell agreement

The will itself has limitations in connection with tax saving, since the most effective techniques must be accomplished during life. Some ideas, however, can be suggested by the accountant:

- Leaving property in trust, particularly to avoid doubling up the estate of the surviving spouse
- Leaving property so that a generation is skipped
- Charitable bequests
- Appropriate provisions qualifying for use of the Marital Deduction
- An appropriate common disaster provision

Advise the Client to Leave Instructions in Addition to the Will

The will is a formal legal document drafted for the purpose of leaving the decedent's property in the manner he wishes. It must be clearly and precisely worded. It should not be cluttered up with provisions of a personal nature.

Personal advice and instructions to the executor and family should be provided in addition to the provisions of the will itself. These take the form of a memo covering a number of points, some examples of which are listed below:

- Suggestions as to investment philosophy and conservation of capital
- Suggestions as to sources of income for living expenses
- Selection of insurance options
- Explanation of the purpose of certain will provisions
- Names of the people to turn to for advice and assistance
- Explantion of where various records can be located
- Explantion of the nature and location of certain assets
- Explanation of the terms of certain debts
- Suggestions as to what to do with certain assets

This type of advice can be very important and helpful to family members who are not well informed as to the client's business affairs. A memo covering points described above gives the client an opportunity to inform family members of his wishes in particular matters, as well as filling in valuable information for the heirs and representatives.

In this same vein, the client should keep his wife as well informed as possible about their business affairs. The writer has seen far too many widows at a complete loss after the death of the husband. Both spouses usually must share the blame for this; the husband has been too busy to take time to keep his wife informed, and she has shown little interest in the business side of their life.

The accountant should urge the client to keep his wife informed by having her take care of certain records or whatever would serve best in the circumstances.

SERVICES AFTER DEATH OF CLIENT OR SPOUSE

The accountant's services become particularly important following the client's death. There will be extra responsibility regarding disposition of the professional practice, as well as a need to set up accounting for the estate. The accountant will also be involved in post-mortem tax planning and advice regarding financial planning.

It is important to be in touch with the family, attorney, and fiduciaries promptly. The accountant should take the initiative to get action underway. Some clients are inclined to put off tax and accounting matters, while others are not aware of what they need to do. Unless the accountant takes the initiative, important matters may be delayed.

Accounting and Income Tax Reporting for the Estate

The extent of formal accounting for estates is mostly determined by state law—some states require formal reporting to a court and some do not. All estates, however, are required to file income tax returns. The accountant must advise regarding accounting for income and expenses of the estate, planning the best tax timing of distributions of income to beneficiaries, and preparation of fiduciary income tax returns.

Service during this period will include preparation of decedent's final income tax return and planning for the manner in which certain items of income and expenses should be reported. Family members and executors are not always familiar with the need to allocate various income and deductions between beneficiaries, the estate, and the decedent's final income tax return. The accountant is the person who needs to keep everyone straight.

Preparation of Estate Tax and Inheritance Tax Returns

It will be necessary to decide who will have responsibility for preparing the estate tax return. Such returns are prepared by bank trust departments, lawyers, and accountants. The person best qualified to do so should be given this responsibility, and in most cases this is the accountant.

An estate tax return is basically a financial statement, and the accountant has the most financial information available on the decedent. He usually has a long history of dealing with the decedent's financial affairs and can gather the necessary data with the least amount of time and effort.

One of the most important reasons for the accountant to prepare the estate tax return is so that all tax work is coordinated. The estate tax valuations have a bearing on future income tax reporting, and the accountant is best situated to understand the relationship between the two. Further, certain deductions can be claimed on either the income tax return or estate tax return, and again the accountant can best coordinate these decisions by doing all the tax work. In most cases the tax work is the most important aspect of estate administration, and it is in the client's best interest to have all tax work handled by the accountant so that it is fully coordinated.

The accountant should take the initiative in making arrangements with the client or his representative concerning preparation of the estate tax return. If the accountant waits to be approached, someone else may assume this responsibility. He should make arrangements in advance, seeking out a suitable opportunity to speak to the client, family, or representative concerning the preparation of the return. Most clients assume that the accountant will prepare the estate tax return, since he has prepared all their other tax returns. When given a choice, this is usually their preference.

In this connection, it is well for the accountant to have an arrangement with lawyers with whom he works regularly regarding the preparation of estate tax returns for mutual clients. If the lawyer prepares these returns, the two are in competition in this aspect of their work. This competition should not impede the professional relationship, however, and it shouldn't be allowed to interfere with service to the client. The lawyer and accountant can and should work together in estate matters, regardless of who actually prepares the return.

CONCLUSION

Opportunities to perform estate work depend on several factors:

- Training and experience of the practitioner
- Developing a clientele with sufficient resources to be concerned about estate planning
- Being alert for opportunities to perform estate work
- Learning when and how to talk to the client about estate matters

The accountant should keep his clients informed of his interest and expertise in the field. One effective means is the use of the client bulletin, with use of articles such as the one in Exhibit 11-4.

FORM 1040 U. S. INDIVIDUAL INCOME TAX RETURN

CLIENT FILE NO.	Name

Every one who handles a client's tax return (Form 1040) should have an *awareness* of additional services which could be of value to the client. This awareness can come about in talking to the client or in reviewing the return and supporting documents. Place an "X" in the box for each item which should be followed up. Add your initials, suggested implementation date, and comments (if any). When the 1040 is completed, this notice is to be forwarded to partners responsible.

Service Items	Suggested By (Initials/Date)	Comments
☐ Estate planning, gifts, trusts updating, wills, consultation, etc.		
☐ Tax entity change—incorporation, Subchapter S, dissolution, etc.		
☐ Clifford trust		
☐ Salary to children		
☐ Family partnership		
☐ Tax shelter investments		
☐ Tax-free bond investments		
☐ Amend prior year returns—additions deductions, net operating loss carrybacks, etc.		
☐ Professional corporation		
☐ Corporate retirement plan		
☐ KEOGH Plan		
☐ I. R. A.		
☐ Set up accounting records or system of recording tax data.		
☐ Other (Describe) _____		

Additional Notes:

_____

_____

_ _

FOLLOW-UP:

_____

_____

_____

Exhibit 11-1: Supplemental Service Worksheet

_____
Date Prepared

Your name _____ Wife's name _____

Home address _____

Your date of birth _____ Wife's date of birth _____

Occupation _____ Date of marriage _____

Names and ages of children, grandchildren, and/or other heirs:

Children	Age	Approximate estate	Grandchildren
_____	____	_____	_____
_____	____	_____	_____
_____	____	_____	_____
_____	____	_____	_____
_____	____	_____	_____
_____	____	_____	_____

Other heirs	Relationship	Age	Approximate estate
_____	_____	____	_____
_____	_____	____	_____
_____	_____	____	_____
_____	_____	____	_____

Current cash flow:

_____	$ _____	$ _____
_____	_____	_____
_____	_____	_____
_____	_____	_____
Income taxes	_____	_____
Living expenses	_____	_____
Balance for investment		$ _____

Exhibit 11-2: Estate Planning Questionnaire

ASSETS

(If ownership is separate, indicate how and when property was acquired)

| | Ownership | | Current value |
	Separate	Community	

Cash

Checking account $ _____ $ _____ $ _____

Savings account   _____   _____   _____

Other   _____   _____   _____

Accounts and notes receivable (describe)

_____   _____   _____   _____

_____   _____   _____   _____

_____   _____   _____   _____

_____   _____   _____   _____

_____   _____   _____   _____

Securities

Stocks-traded, at cost or tax basis:

No. of
shares   Description

Exhibit 11-2: Estate Planning Questionaire (Continued)

ASSETS (Continued)

Bonds, at cost or tax basis:

Par value	Description			
_____	_____	_____	_____	_____
_____	_____	_____	_____	_____
_____	_____	_____	_____	_____
_____	_____	_____	_____	_____
_____	_____	_____	_____	_____
_____	_____	_____	_____	_____
_____	_____	_____	_____	_____
_____	_____	_____	_____	_____

	Ownership		Current
	Separate	Community	value

Real estate, at cost or tax basis:

_____	_____	_____	_____
_____	_____	_____	_____
_____	_____	_____	_____
_____	_____	_____	_____
_____	_____	_____	_____

Mineral interest, at cost or tax basis:

_____	_____	_____	_____
_____	_____	_____	_____
_____	_____	_____	_____
_____	_____	_____	_____
_____	_____	_____	_____
_____	_____	_____	_____
_____	_____	_____	_____

Exhibit 11-2: Estate Planning Questionaire (Continued)

ASSETS (Continued)

<u>(If ownership is separate, indicate how and when property was acquired)</u>

	Separate	Community	Current value
Business interests			
Individual proprietorship – net worth	_____	_____	_____
Interest in partnership – net worth	_____	_____	_____
Stock in close corporation – cost or other tax basis	_____	_____	_____

Pension and profit-sharing plans, stock options, deferred compensation agreements (describe and indicate beneficiary provisions) _____

_____

_____

_____

Interest in trusts established by others, including powers of appointment (give details) _____

_____

_____

_____

<u>Personal Property, at current value</u>

	Separate	Community	Current value
Household furnishings	_____	_____	_____
Automobiles	_____	_____	_____

Other (describe):

	Separate	Community	Current value
_____	_____	_____	_____
_____	_____	_____	_____
_____	_____	_____	_____
_____	_____	_____	_____

Exhibit 11-2: Estate Planning Questionnaire (Continued)

ASSETS (Continued)

<u>Life Insurance</u>

Insurance
company

_____ _____ _____ _____ _____

_____ _____ _____ _____ _____

_____ _____ _____ _____ _____

Policy #   _____ _____ _____ _____ _____

Date of policy _____ _____ _____ _____ _____

Type of policy _____ _____ _____ _____ _____

_____ _____ _____ _____ _____

Face amount _____ _____ _____ _____ _____

_____ _____ _____ _____ _____

Owner   _____ _____ _____ _____ _____

Beneficiary _____ _____ _____ _____ _____

Insured   _____ _____ _____ _____ _____

_____ _____ _____ _____ _____

Cash surrender
value   _____ _____ _____ _____ _____

Loans against
policies   _____ _____ _____ _____ _____

_____ _____ _____ _____ _____

<u>Potential inheritances (give details)</u>

_____

_____

_____

_____

_____

_____

Exhibit 11-2: Estate Planning Questionnaire (Continued)

LIABILITIES

	Ownership	
	Separate	Community

Notes payable (describe):

_____   _____ _____
_____   _____ _____
_____   _____ _____
_____   _____ _____

Accounts payable (describe):

_____   _____ _____
_____   _____ _____
_____   _____ _____

Mortgages (describe):

_____   _____ _____
_____   _____ _____
_____   _____ _____

Other liabilities, including
  contingent (explain):

_____   _____ _____
_____   _____ _____

OTHER INFORMATION REQUIRED

1. Copies of wills of husband and wife
2. Prior gift tax returns, unless prepared by us
3. Federal income tax returns for last three years unless prepared by us
4. Copies of trust agreements in which you or your wife are donor or beneficiary, or under which either of you have powers of appointment
5. Buy-and-sell agreements
6. Current financial statements of business interests
7. Insurance policies
8. Partnership agreements

Exhibit 11-2: Estate Planning Questionaire (Continued)

THE WILL QUIZ

A YES answer to any of the following questions could be a danger signal. There are gift tax returns, new Wills and Estate Planning which should be considered:

	YES	NO
1. You or your spouse does not have a will?	☐	☐
2. Have any beneficiaries named in your will died since the will was drawn?	☐	☐
3. Have any beneficiaries become (since the will was drawn) more capable—or less capable—of managing their money and investments?	☐	☐
4. Have children or grandchildren been born since your will was drawn?	☐	☐
5. Does your will make gifts of specific property that you no longer own, or that has changed in character?	☐	☐
6. Have any of the beneficiaries named in your will married since your will was drawn?	☐	☐
7. Have you moved from one state to another since your will was drawn?	☐	☐
8. Has the total value of your assets changed substantially since your will was drawn?	☐	☐
9. Have you taken out more life insurance since your will was drawn?	☐	☐
10. Have you become a participant in retirement plans or other fringe benefit programs provided by your employer company?	☐	☐
11. Have you and another person put any property in your names jointly, with right of survivorship?	☐	☐
12. Was your will drawn a long time ago, before certain important changes were made in the Federal estate and income tax laws?	☐	☐
13. Did you fail this quiz?	☐	☐
14. Do you refuse to do something about it...NOW?	☐	☐

Exhibit 11-3: The Will Quiz

THE NEED FOR ESTATE PLANNING

An increasing number of people are recognizing the importance of a carefully prepared estate plan. Such plans provide better security and benefits for family members and hold inheritance taxes to the lowest possible level. Anyone should be in a position to answer the following questions:

How much am I worth at this time?

What is the potential size of my estate, considering life insurance proceeds?

How much will estate taxes and administration costs amount to?

Will there be enough cash available to meet all the needs?

Are the beneficiaries of my estate capable of handling it once it is in their hands?

Is my will up-to-date and does it actually do the job as intended?

Often after an estate plan has been prepared it is assumed that the job is completed. Unfortunately, however, numerous changes occur over the years that cause these plans to become obsolete. The plan should be reviewed, therefore, from time to time. Some of the changes that can make the plan obsolete are:

Marriage of a child

Death of a child

Death of a spouse

Ill health of child or spouse

Significant increase or decrease in net worth

Significant change in type of property owned

Significant change in business relationship with partners or others

Many people prefer to ignore estate planning. This can create problems among family members and can become very expensive. If you have not faced up to this situation we urge you to do so.

Exhibit 11-4: Client Bulletin

Index